PORTUG AL TRAVEL GUIDE 2024

The Comprehensive And Updated Travel Guide To Explore Spain And Portugal like a Local, Everything You Need To Know

KEVIN M. STAPLES

Copyright © 2024 by Kevin M. Staples

Table of contents

INTRODUCTION TO SPAIN AND PORTUGAL

I felt a surge of exhilaration as I got off the aircraft in Madrid and felt the warm Spanish sun kissing my face. For as long as I could remember, I had always wanted to go to Spain and Portugal, and now my dream was coming true.

My first trip was to Madrid, a city renowned for its lively energy and extensive cultural offerings. My ears were filled with the sweet sounds of Spanish conversations as I went through the city's cobblestone streets, my eyes feasting on the gorgeous architecture. A reminder of Spain's regal past, the regal Palace was stately and intimidating.

One evening, I went to a classic tapas bar where both residents and visitors congregated to enjoy delectable tapas. When I experienced foods like jamón ibérico and patatas bravas, the flavors erupted in my tongue. I couldn't help but participate in the vibrant discussions going on around me, and soon I began to feel like a thread in Spanish life's tapestry.

I took a train from Madrid to Seville, where I immediately fell in love with the city's charming streets and passionate flamenco performances. I took a stroll inside Seville's Alcázar, a palace that had the feel of a fantasy setting. I knew I was in a slice of heaven when the aroma of orange blossoms permeated the air.

Lisbon was my next stop as Portugal beckoned. I was

welcomed by the city's vibrant tiles and vintage trams as it nestled on seven hills. The panoramic view of the city and the Tagus River below astounded me as I stood at the Miradouro da Senhora do Monte.

A quick train trip to Sintra took me to a magical world full of castles. I wandered the Palacio Nacional da Pena's gardens as if in a dream since they were a kaleidoscope of hues.

I traveled to Porto in the north, exploring the quaint alleys of the Ribeira neighborhood and the elegant Douro River. In the cellars that lined the riverbanks, I had some port wine and experienced the kind welcome of the locals.

My adventure across Portugal continued at the academic town of Coimbra, where the ethereally lovely Fado music filled the air and its melancholy melodies touched my soul.

I was astonished by the Alhambra Palace in Granada

when I returned to Spain. I couldn't help but be in awe of the complex Moorish architecture and the Generalife Gardens.

My last stop was Barcelona, a place where the ancient and the modern coexist together. I was in awe of Antoni Gaud's fanciful creations and had a feeling of youthful delight as I wandered around Park Güell and the Sagrada Familia.

I thought back on the amazing trip I had just had as I got on the aircraft to go home. With their beauty, culture, and friendliness, Spain and Portugal had won my heart. I couldn't wait to tell my friends and family the tales and experiences I had on this trip since I knew I would cherish them forever. It had been a complete dream come true for me to make my first trip to these beautiful nations, and I was thankful for every second of it.

Welcome To Spain

Spain is a stunningly beautiful nation with a wide variety of landscapes that engage the senses and astound visitors. Spain's natural and man-made treasures come together to form a visual tapestry that is nothing short of magnificent, from the imposing mountains to the peaceful coasts, from the ancient towns to the charming countryside.

Magnificent Mountains:

The Pyrenees, a magnificent mountain range in the northeast, entices hikers, skiers, and nature lovers with its snow-capped peaks, verdant valleys, and crystal-clear lakes. The towering mountains of the southern Sierra Nevada, which includes Mulhacén, the highest peak on the Iberian Peninsula, provide a striking contrast. These mountains not only provide exhilarating outdoor activities but also kilometers of stunning views.

Coastline Paradise:
The lengthy coastline of Spain offers a wide variety of sceneries. You can discover stunning beaches with golden sand and sparkling seas all around the Mediterranean coast. The year-round sunlight and beach resorts on the Costa del Sol and Costa Blanca are well-known. The northern shore, however, has a distinct beauty with its verdant greenery, towering cliffs, and quaint fishing towns. Particularly the Bay of Biscay offers breathtaking vistas of the Atlantic Ocean.

Interesting Islands:
The islands of Spain are strewn over the ocean like undiscovered pearls. A Mediterranean paradise with immaculate beaches, clear oceans, and attractive towns can be found in the Balearic Islands, which include Mallorca, Ibiza, and Menorca. In contrast, the Canary Islands, which sit off

the coast of northwest Africa, are a volcanic paradise with a variety of landscapes, from Lanzarote's lunar-like topography to La Gomera's lush woods. These islands provide distinctive ecosystems and natural marvels in addition to being aesthetically stunning.

Historic cities include:

Cities in Spain are a fascinating fusion of the past and the present. The city, of Madrid, is home to opulent boulevards, charming squares, and top-notch museums like the Prado. The magnificent Sagrada Familia is only one example of Antoni Gaud's captivating combination of imagination and reality in Barcelona's architecture. Seville has a timeless allure with its Alcazar, which has Moorish influences, and its busy streets. The Alhambra Palace in Granada is a marvel of Islamic architecture situated against the Sierra Nevada. It is a UNESCO World Heritage Site.

Beautiful countryside

If you explore the countryside of Spain, you'll find picture-perfect towns, undulating hills, vineyards, and olive groves. The areas of Andalusia, known for its white-washed towns, and La Rioja, well-known for its wines, are just a few examples of the country's many beautiful rural settings. Driving slowly through sunflower fields and taking strolls along cobblestone paths are encouraged by the Spanish countryside.

Parks and natural reserves:

Also abundant in Spain are parks and natural reserves like Donana National Park and Ordesa y Monte Perdido National Park. These protected areas are home to distinctive ecosystems, such as marshes, woodlands, and a variety of species, providing a chance to appreciate the beauty of nature.

The majesty of Spain's mountains, the tranquility of

its coasts, the depth of its history, and the charm of its communities all contribute to the country's diverse and ever-evolving beauty. It is a place where the senses are heightened, where beauty can be found around every corner, and where visitors are left with lingering recollections of a place that can captivate the soul.

CHAPTER 1

The interesting facts about Spain

Spain has a lot to offer visitors, from its breathtaking countryside and idyllic beaches to its rich history and culture. Here are just a few intriguing facts about Spain:

The beaches: There are plenty of beaches to pick from in Spain because of its more than 8,000 kilometers of coastline. You are sure to discover the ideal location to unwind and enjoy the sun, whether you're searching for a quiet cove or a bustling resort beach. The Playa de Ses Illetes in Formentera, the Playa de la Concha in San Sebastián, and the Playa de Bolonia in Cádiz are a few of the most well-known beaches in Spain.

Spain offers some of the world's liveliest and most stunning cities. The capital, Madrid, is a multicultural city with a flourishing arts and entertainment scene. **Barcelona is renowned for its beautiful architecture and exciting nightlife**. Seville is a lovely city with a Moorish background. Valencia, Granada, and Bilbao are a few of the other well-known cities in Spain.

The food: Spanish cuisine is renowned for its use of fresh ingredients and its variety of tastes. Tapas, paella, and tortilla Espanola are a few of the most well-known Spanish foods. and also Some of the world's top wines may be found in Spain.

Spain has a vibrant and diversified culture. The nation is renowned for its music, dancing, and visual arts. Spanish music and dance known as flamenco has its roots in Andalusia. Pop, rock, and classical music are some other popular music genres in Spain. Spain is also home to numerous internationally famous museums, like the Prado Museum in Madrid and the Picasso Museum in Barcelona.

The background: Spain has a lengthy and intriguing past. The Roman Empire, the Visigoths, and the Moors all formerly resided in the nation. Spain's architecture, culture, and food all reflect its rich legacy. The Alhambra in Granada, the Sagrada Familia in Barcelona, and the Mezquita in Cordoba are a few of the most well-known historical landmarks in Spain.

In addition to all of these incredible things, Spain is also a very friendly and reasonably priced destination. The people are welcoming, and living expenses are not too high. Because of this, Spain is a fantastic location for tourists and visitors of various financial means.

Here are a few other details that make Spain amazing:

The Canary Islands: These volcanic islands off the coast of Africa are well-liked vacation spots because of their breathtaking beauty, comfortable climate, and black sand beaches.

The Balearic Islands: These Mediterranean Sea islands are renowned for their stunning beaches, azure oceans, and exciting nightlife.

The Picos de Europa: This mountain range in northern Spain is well-liked for trekking, camping, and skiing.

Whatever your hobbies, Spain is certain to have something you'll adore. Everyone can find

something to like in our
nation.

Geography Of Spain

With a vast variety of
landscapes and natural
features, Spain's geography
is as fascinating as it is
varied. Spain's geography
may be generally divided
into several different areas,
all of which are located on
the Iberian Peninsula in
southwest Europe:

1. Mountains: The Pyrenees
mountain range forms a
natural barrier along Spain's
northern border with France.
These mountains are a
refuge for outdoor
enthusiasts and hikers
because of their craggy
summits, deep valleys, and
crystal-clear lakes.

2. plateaus The meseta, a
huge central plateau that
spans most of the nation,
dominates Spain's heartland.
The meseta is a high, flat
area of terrain that offers
expansive views and
stretches of rolling plains.

Spain's central region is notable for the Castilian Plateau, which is a component of the Meseta.

3. Coastal areas With the Mediterranean Sea to its east and the Atlantic Ocean to its north and northwest, Spain has a varied coastline. With golden sands and crystal-clear waves, the Mediterranean coast is renowned for its gorgeous beaches. The northern shore, in contrast, is distinguished by impressive cliffs, rich vegetation, and beautiful fishing communities.

4. Islands: There are various archipelagos in Spain, the most notable of which being the Canary Islands (Tenerife, Gran Canaria, Lanzarote, etc.) and the Balearic Islands (Mallorca, Ibiza, Menorca, etc.) off the northwest coast of Africa. These islands provide a diverse array of topographies, from lush woods and gorgeous beaches to volcanic mountains.

5. Deserts: The southeasterly district of

Almera is renowned for its scenery that resembles the semi-desert. The Tabernas Desert, which is located in this area, stands out for its distinct dry beauty and has even served as the setting for several well-known Western movies.

6. Rivers: The Ebro, Tagus (Tajo), Guadalquivir, and Duero (Douro) are just a few of the significant rivers that flow through Spain. As they pass through diverse areas, these rivers sculpt the landscape and sustain ecosystems and agriculture.

7. Parks that are natural: Spain is dedicated to protecting its natural beauty, and there are several parks and reserves around the country. While Donana National Park is a large swamp teeming with species, the Picos de Europa in the north has striking limestone peaks. Diverse flora and wildlife may find a home in these protected regions.

8. The Canary Islands, in particular, Lanzarote, are

well-known for their volcanic topography. The Timanfaya National Park in Lanzarote exhibits a bizarre, extraterrestrial landscape created by previous volcanic explosions.

Spain's topography, in general, is a monument to its richness, providing a broad selection of outdoor adventures and natural marvels for those who explore its different landscapes. Spain's geographical diversity, which ranges from towering mountains to gorgeous coasts, from deserts to lush plains, adds to its appeal as a mesmerizing and aesthetically appealing nation.

Climate Of Spain

Due to its wide geographic span and varying topography, Spain has a highly diversified climate. The nation enjoys a broad variety of climatic conditions, from the

Mediterranean in the coastal districts to deserts in the southeast, and even alpine in the mountainous regions. Here is a summary of Spain's climate:

1. Regions with a Mediterranean climate include: The majority of Spain's coastal regions, including the eastern and southern shores, have a Mediterranean climate.

These areas have warm, dry summers and moderate, rainy winters. Winters are pleasant, with temperatures seldom dropping below freezing, while summers are normally bright with regular highs of 30°C (86°F). Rainfall mostly occurs in the colder months.

2. Continental Climate:

Regions: Spain's central heartland, which includes the Meseta plateau and places around Madrid, has a continental climate.

The temperature in this area varies more from season to season. Winters may be chilly with occasional snowfall, but summers are often hot and dry, sometimes exceeding 35°C (95°F). Low and erratic rainfall is the norm.

3. Atlantic Climate

areas: Spain's northern coast and northwest areas, including Galicia and Asturias, enjoy an Atlantic climate.

These regions have pleasant summers with temperatures of 20–25°C (68–77°F) and a moderately high humidity level. The cold and damp winters seldom see temperatures below freezing. Rainfall is equally distributed throughout the year, creating lush, verdant landscapes.

4. Arid Climate:

The southeast of Spain, notably the Almera area and portions of Murcia, has an arid or semi-arid climate. Summers in this area are exceptionally hot and dry, with frequent highs of 40 °C (104 °F). Although the winters are warm and dry, when they do rain, it may be rather heavy. This region often experiences droughts.

5. Mountain and Alpine Climate: Spain's mountainous areas, such as the Pyrenees and the Sierra Nevada, have an alpine climate at higher altitudes.

Mountain summers are milder, with average highs of 20°C (68°F). Winters are chilly and snowy, with lows below zero. Higher elevations often see precipitation in the form of snow.

6. Canary Islands Climate: Regions:The Canary Islands, which are off the northwest coast of Africa, have a subtropical climate. There is minimal seasonal change on these islands' moderate temperatures. Winters are delightfully moderate, seldom falling below 15°C (59°F), while summers are warm, averaging approximately 25-30°C (77-86°F). Conditions are dry to semi-arid since rainfall varies per island but is typically insufficient.

Because of its diverse climate, visitors are drawn to Spain all year round. Spain's diverse climates provide a selection of experiences to suit every desire, whether you're looking for sunny beaches, chilly mountain getaways, or culturally vibrant towns.

Culture Of Spanish

A vibrant tapestry of tradition and modernity weaves together Spanish culture.

Spain's culture is an alluring fusion of illustrious traditions, imaginative creative expression, and a zeal for living that infuses every facet of everyday life. Spanish culture, which is rooted in its history, geography, and different people, is a celebration of both the ancient and the contemporary.

Language:
The foundation of Spain's cultural identity is the Spanish language,

commonly known as Castilian. With regional variants that represent the linguistic variety of the country, it is widely spoken throughout. You may also hear regional tongues like Catalan, Valencian, and Basque in places like Catalonia, Valencia, and the Basque Country.

Cuisine:

The robust tastes and geographical variety of Spanish cuisine are well-known around the globe. Valencia is the place where paella, a rice dish flavored with saffron, first appeared. Small plates of savory foods called tapas promote social eating and provide a variety of flavors and textures. A long legacy of winemaking, with places like Rioja producing some of the world's best wines, as well as mouthwatering hams like jamón ibérico and gazpacho are all part of Spain's rich culinary heritage.

Festivals and celebrations include:

Spanish people are renowned for their boisterous festivals and festivities, which are steeped in history and draw on the nation's many cultural influences. The somber but aesthetically stunning religious celebration known as Semana Santa, or Holy Week, is celebrated throughout Spain with processions and pomp. La Tomatina in Bunol has a sizable tomato battle that draws tourists from all around the globe. Despite its unpopularity, bullfighting is nevertheless a part of Spanish culture, especially in areas like Andalusia.

Flamenco:

Spanish culture is frequently referred to as having its heart and soul in flamenco, a passionate and emotional art form. Flamenco, which has its roots in Andalusia, blends singing (cante), dancing (baile), and playing the guitar (toque) to emote strongly. It's a visceral representation of life's pleasures and tragedies; it's not simply an act.

Visual Arts and Architecture:

The world has been forever changed by Spain's creative achievements. Spanish-born visionary artists who have significantly influenced the field of art include Pablo Picasso and Salvador Dali. The Sagrada Familia in Barcelona is one of architect Antoni Gaud's fanciful works that is praised for its original and inventive features. The varied heritage of the nation is reflected in historical sites like the Alhambra in Granada and the Great Mosque in Cordoba.

Bullfighting:

Bullfighting is still seen as part of Spanish culture, despite being debatable and losing popularity. It has a rich historical background and is often regarded as an art form, with matadors showcasing incredible skill and courage in the arena. Thoughts about animal suffering and other ethical issues still accompany this technique.

Siesta and way of life:

The siesta, a custom of pausing in the middle of the day to rest and avoid the warmest parts of the day, is the embodiment of Spain's laid-back way of life. Through encouraging leisurely meals and a slower pace of life, this practice has impacted daily routines and social interactions.

Social gatherings and fiestas:

Spaniards are renowned for their love of celebration and socializing. In Spain, the idea of a "fiesta" is strongly ingrained, and you may often encounter colorful gatherings, music, and dancing at regional festivals and festivities. These celebratory activities often include street parties, parades, and fireworks.

Religious Traditions:

Grand cathedrals, churches, and religious celebrations in Spain all reflect the country's rich religious tradition. Processions during Semana Santa (Holy Week), which include elaborate demonstrations of religious piety and customary practices, are especially prominent.

The culture of Spain is proof of its capacity to meld the traditional with the modern in a seamless manner. It is a nation where the past is present in every area, where the arts stimulate the imagination, and where people enjoy life to the fullest via cuisine, music, and celebrations. Spain welcomes you to enjoy its diverse and vibrant culture, whether you're tasting tapas, strolling through historical alleys, or losing yourself in the passionate rhythms of Flamenco.

CHAPTER2

Visa Requirements To Visit Spain

Depending on your nationality, the reason for your trip, and how long you want to stay, you may need a visa to enter Spain. Spain is a member of the Schengen Area, which enables passport-free travel among its participating nations. The following general information about Spanish visa requirements is provided:

1. Schengen Visa: If you are a citizen of a nation that is not a member of the European Union (EU) or the European Economic Area (EEA), you will normally require a Schengen Visa to enter Spain for brief stays (up to 90 days within 180 days).

All Schengen Area participants, including Spain, are eligible for the Schengen

Visa. So, if you receive a Schengen Visa from one Schengen nation, you may travel to Spain and other Schengen nations while there.

2. Visa Exemptions: For brief stays, several nations are excluded from getting a Schengen Visa. It is not necessary to get a visa to visit Spain or the Schengen Area for up to 90 days within 180 days if you are a citizen of certain nations, including the United States, Canada, Australia, and many others. This exemption, however, does not apply if you want to work or study in Spain.

3. Long-Term Visas and Residence Permits:
You will normally need to apply for a long-term visa or residence permit before your arrival if you want to remain in Spain for more than 90 days for reasons like job, education, or family reunion. Depending on why you are visiting, different criteria and

application procedures apply.

4. Transit Visa: Depending on your nationality, you may need an airport transit visa if you are passing through a Spanish airport on your route to another country. A transit visa at an airport is not necessary for brief layovers, nevertheless, for nationals of many different nations.

5. Visa Application Process: You must ordinarily apply at the Spanish consulate or embassy in your home country to get a long-term visa or a Schengen visa. A valid passport, a completed visa application form, a trip itinerary, proof of lodging, evidence of financial capability, and additional criteria depending on the reason for your visit are normally required throughout the application process.

6. Biometric Data Collection: At the visa application center, embassy, or consulate, you can be asked to provide biometric information, such as your fingerprints, as part of the visa application procedure.

Please be aware that visa requirements and exemptions can change over time, so it is crucial to check the official website of the Spanish Ministry of Foreign Affairs or speak with the Spanish embassy or consulate in your country for the most recent and detailed information regarding your visa requirements and application process. It's also a good idea to start the visa application procedure well in advance of your intended trip to Spain.

Basic Things To Know Before Visiting Spain

Important Information to Consider Before Traveling to Spain
Spain is a popular destination for tourists from all over the globe because of its rich cultural history,

breathtaking scenery, and bustling towns. It's crucial to educate yourself with some fundamental knowledge about Spain before you go there to make sure your vacation is pleasurable and respectful of local culture. The main details you need to be aware of are as follows:

1. Language:

The official language of Spain is Spanish, sometimes known as Castilian (Castellano). Although many Spaniards in tourist destinations and large cities understand English, it is always appreciated when visitors attempt to converse in Spanish. It might be quite beneficial to learn a few simple words and phrases.

2. Currency:

Euro (€) Spain's official currency is the euro. Make sure to convert your money into euros before or when you arrive, and acquaint yourself with the current exchange rates.

3. Safety and Health: Spain is typically a safe nation for tourists. But just like anyplace else, you must exercise fundamental safety procedures, such as protecting your possessions and paying attention to your surroundings. Although Spain offers first-rate medical facilities, it is nevertheless important to get travel insurance that covers unforeseen costs and medical emergencies.

4. Time Zone: Spain lies in the Central European Time (CET) zone, which runs from UTC+1 during normal time to UTC+2 during daylight saving time.

5.   Tipping Etiquette: Tipping is usual in Spain but not as generously as in some other nations. In restaurants, it's customary to offer a modest tip, either rounding up the total or leaving between 5 and 10%. While leaving modest change is appreciated, tipping is less frequent at pubs and cafés. It's normal to provide tips to hotel and transportation employees.

6. Siesta custom number: The siesta is a customary break in the early afternoon when many stores, companies, and even some restaurants shut for a while. Even while this custom is less common in major cities and tourist hotspots, it's important to be aware of possible closures during siesta time in smaller villages.

7. Dining Culture: Spaniards have a distinctive dining culture with late mealtimes. The time for lunch, or "comida," is usually between 1:30 and 3:30 PM, while the time for supper, or "cena," is usually 8:30 or later. Take advantage of the tapas culture and experience Spain's delectable cuisine.

8. Festivals & Events: Spain is renowned for its exuberant festivities and festivals. The country's rich cultural legacy is celebrated during Semana

Santa (Holy Week), La Tomatina, and various regional fiestas. To learn whether any festivals are taking place during your stay, check the neighborhood event calendar.

9. Respect for Local Customs and Traditions: Show respect for regional traditions and customs, particularly at places of worship and while attending cultural events. When visiting churches and cathedrals, dress modestly and observe any applicable dress and conduct codes.

10. Spain has a robust and effective public transportation system that includes trains, buses, trams, and metros in major cities. For convenience and cost savings, think about acquiring transit cards or passes.

11. Regional Diversity: Spain is a diversified nation with several regions, each of which has its own culture, customs, and food. Discover the distinct attractions of regions like Catalonia, Andalusia, the Basque Country, and others by venturing outside of the big cities.

You'll be ready to enjoy a great and culturally enriching experience when visiting Spain if you bear these fundamental truths in mind. Spain has something to offer any tourist looking to experience its thriving culture and spectacular scenery, whether they're meandering through old districts, unwinding on gorgeous beaches, or indulging in tasty tapas.

Best Time To Visit Spain for the best experience

Selecting the Best Time to Visit Spain for the Best Experience

The date of your journey to Spain might have a big influence on how enjoyable it will be. It is crucial to choose the optimal season for your interests and preferences since this beautiful nation provides a broad variety of temperatures, landscapes, and cultural activities all year long. Here is a guide to assist you in selecting the ideal season to go to Spain for an amazing experience:

1. Spring (March to May): Weather: Springtime temperatures in Spain are normally warm, averaging between 15°C and 25°C (59°F and 77°F).

- Exposure to another culture via springtime celebrations, such as the magnificent Semana Santa (Holy Week) processions.
- Beaches are less busy than they were at the height of the summer.

2. Summer (June to August): Weather: Summers are often hot and sunny, with temperatures rising to 30°C to 40°C (86°F to 104°F) on occasion.

- Perfect for beach holidays in locales like the Balearic Islands and the Costa de
- More daylight hours for outdoor excursions and prolonged touring Bustling fairs, concerts, and outdoor markets are all going strong.
- Be prepared for high temperatures since inland communities may face sweltering heat.
- Busy tourist areas are congested, and hotel rates might go up.

3. Autumn (September to November):

Weather: Autumn is characterized by comfortable temperatures between 20°C and 30°C (68°F and 86°F), which progressively decrease from summer highs.

- Pleasant weather for outdoor pursuits like

trekking and seeing historical sites.

- The time of year when grapes are harvested in wine areas like La Rioja and Catalonia, which is great for wine lovers.
- Tourist hotspots that are less crowded as the summer season winds down.
- Distinctive cultural events, like La Mercè in Barcelona, provide genuine experiences.
- Periodic rainfall is possible in certain areas, especially in the north.

4. Winter (December to February): Weather: Many parts of Spain endure a warm winter with temperatures between 8°C and 15°C (46°F and 59°F). There may be snowfall in mountainous areas.

- Without the summertime throngs, it's perfect for city sightseeing, museum visits, and historical site excursions.

- The Pyrenees and Sierra Nevada are ideal locations for skiers and snowboarders.
- Seasonal festivals and marketplaces in cities like Madrid and Barcelona.
- Coastal areas may have colder and rainier weather.
- Some tourist sites may have shortened hours or closures, particularly in smaller towns.

The ideal time to go to Spain mostly depends on your interests and the experiences you want to have, to sum up. The best seasons are often thought to be spring and fall since they provide comfortable weather, fewer visitors, and a wide variety of indoor and outdoor activities.

Basic Spanish phrase to interact with the locals

Interacting with locals in their native language is a great way to enhance your travel experience in Spain. While many Spaniards in tourist areas speak English, making an effort to speak Spanish can be appreciated. Here are some basic Spanish phrases to help you connect with locals:

1. Hello:
English: Hello
Spanish: Hola (Oh-lah)

2. Good morning:
English: Good morning
Spanish: Buenos días (Bway-nos dee-ahs)

3. Good afternoon/evening:
English: Good afternoon/evening
Spanish: Buenas tardes (Bway-nahs tar-des)

4. Good night:
English: Good night
Spanish: Buenas noches (Bway-nahs noh-ches)

5. Please:

English: Please
Spanish: Por favor (Por fah-vor)

6. Thank you:
English: Thank you
Spanish: Gracias (Grah-see-ahs)

7. You're welcome:
English: You're welcome
Spanish: De nada (Deh nah-dah)

8. Excuse me / Sorry:
English: Excuse me / Sorry
Spanish: Perdón (Pair-don)

9. Yes:
English: Yes
Spanish: Sí (See)

10. No:
English: No
Spanish: No (No)

11. I don't understand:
English: I don't understand
Spanish: No entiendo (Noh en-tee-en-doh)

12. I'm lost:
English: I'm lost
Spanish: Estoy perdido (Es-toy pair-dee-doh) [if you're male
Estoy perdida (Estoy pair-dee-dah) [if you're female]

13. How much does this cost?:

English: How much does this cost?
Spanish: ¿Cuánto cuesta esto? (Kwan-to kwes-ta es-to)

14. Where is...?:
English: Where is...?
Spanish: ¿Dónde está...? (Dón-de es-ta...?)

15. I need help:
English: I need help
Spanish: Necesito ayuda (Neh-seh-see-toh ah-yoo-dah)

16. Water:
English: Water
Spanish: Agua (Ah-gwah)

17. Food:
English: Food
Spanish: Comida (Koh-mee-dah)

18. Bathroom / Toilet:
English: Bathroom / Toilet
Spanish: Baño (Bahn-yoh)

19. I'm vegetarian:
English: I'm vegetarian
Spanish: Soy vegetariano (Soy veh-heh-tah-ree-ah-no) [if you're male]
Soy vegetariana (Soy veh-heh-tah-ree-ah) [if you're female]

20. I'm allergic to...:

English: I'm allergic to…
Spanish: Soy alérgico/a a...
(Soy ah-lehr-hee-koh/ah ah...)

Remember that pronunciation is key, so practice these phrases to feel more confident while interacting with locals. Spanish speakers often appreciate the effort you make to speak their language, even if it's just a few basic phrases.

Things To Bring Along On Your Trip To Spain

Planning a trip to Spain, whether it's for a city break in Barcelona, a beach holiday on the Costa del Sol, or a cultural tour of Madrid, involves careful packing to guarantee smooth and pleasurable travel. Here is a thorough list of everything you must pack for your trip to Spain to aid in your preparation:

1. Passport and Travel Documents

Check that your passport is valid for at least six months after the date you want to travel.

Make copies of crucial papers, such as your passport, travel insurance, and visa (if necessary), and keep them separate from the originals.

2. Money and Payment Methods: Bring a combination of Euros in cash for little needs and cards for bigger purchases.

To prevent card problems overseas, let your bank know about your vacation intentions.

Your cash and credit cards may be kept secure with a money belt or a travel wallet.

3. Travel Insurance: It's crucial to have comprehensive travel insurance that addresses theft, trip cancellation, and medical situations.

Carry a physical or digital copy of your insurance policy.

4. Prescription prescriptions and First Aid

Kit: Be sure to include plenty of any necessary prescription prescriptions.

Pack a basic first aid bag with all the necessary supplies, such as bandages, painkillers, antiseptic wipes, and any personal medical goods.

5. Power Adapter and Voltage Converter:

Electrical outlets in Spain are of the Type C and Type F European design, and the voltage is 220-240V. Bring the proper adapters and voltage converters, if necessary.

6. A travel manual or digital travel software may assist you in navigating Spain's sights and culture.

Maps of the cities and areas you want to visit, whether printed or digital, might be useful.

7. Language essentials

Include a pocket-sized English-Spanish phrasebook or language-learning software that may make it easier to communicate with natives.

For convenience, think about using offline translation applications.

8. Travel backpack or daypack:

A cozy, lightweight backpack is perfect for day outings, hauling necessities, and adventuring.

Check that it has safe compartments to prevent pickpocketing.

9. Clothes:

Pack clothes appropriate for the weather and the activities you have planned.

Although Spain's dress code is often informal, you might consider dressing up for nights out in big towns.

If you're traveling to a beach resort, don't forget your swimsuit.

10. Comfy Shoes:

For seeing cities, monuments, and outdoor attractions, comfortable walking shoes or sneakers are a must.

Bring the right shoes if you want to trek.

11. Check the weather prediction before packing

suitable apparel, such as a lightweight jacket, raincoat, or sweater.

A scarf, gloves, and cap might be helpful during the colder months.

12. Toiletries and a Travel Towel

A quick-dry travel towel saves space and is useful for excursions to the beach and hostels.

Bring travel-sized essentials like shampoo, conditioner, soap, toothpaste, and a toothbrush.

13. Sunscreen with a high SPF rating, sunglasses, and a wide-brimmed hat are essential for sun protection in Spain's bright environment.

Additionally beneficial can be insect repellant.

14. Adapters for gadgets: If you're taking gadgets, be sure you have the right adapters for charging them.

15. Don't forget your smartphone, camera, e-reader, or any other technology you'll need throughout your vacation.

It is crucial to have chargers, power banks, and extra batteries.

16.   Reusable water bottles may help you save money and reduce plastic waste since tap water in Spain is often safe to drink.

17. Luggage locks and security measures
To avoid theft when traveling, secure your bags using TSA-approved locks.

If you want more security in your lodgings, think about getting a portable door lock.

18. Travel Pillow and Earplugs: A travel pillow may make lengthy travels more pleasant.

Noise-canceling headphones or earplugs are beneficial for restful sleep, particularly in busy cities.

19. A backpack rain cover may shield your stuff from the elements during sudden downpours if you're carrying a backpack.

20.   Bring novels, periodicals, or digital entertainment to pass the time on planes, trains, or in downtime.

21. Copies of Important Information:

Keep copies of your passport, itinerary, and travel insurance in a place apart from the originals.

For simple access, store digital copies in cloud storage.

22. trip Journal and Pen: Write down your impressions and recollections in a trip journal.

For writing down notes and completing documents, a pen might be helpful.

You will be well-prepared to take full advantage of your vacation to Spain if you carry these necessary goods. Adapt your packing list to the exact activities and areas you want to visit, and don't forget to allow room for any souvenirs and gems you may find on the route. Have a safe journey!

#CHAPTER 3

Getting Around Spain for the first time of visit

It may be a thrilling experience to travel for the first time in Spain, and traveling about this beautiful and varied nation is usually simple. The bustling cities, charming villages, and breathtaking landscapes of Spain may be explored via several transportation methods. On your first visit, use this road map to go about Spain:

1. Air Travel: If you're coming from outside, you'll probably arrive at one of Spain's main international airports, such as Madrid-Barajas Airport or Barcelona-El Prat Airport. Spain has a vast domestic aircraft network, which makes it easy to travel rapidly across considerable distances. Major cities may easily be reached from regional airports as well.

2. Trains: Spain has an effective and vast high-speed rail network known as the AVE (Alta Velocidad Espanola). Several important cities are connected by these trains, including Madrid, Barcelona, Seville, Valencia, and Malaga. You may simply purchase tickets at train stations or online via Renfe, the country's railroad provider. Traveling by rail is often pleasant and picturesque.

3. Metro and Public Transit: Spain's largest cities, such as Madrid, Barcelona, Valencia, and Seville, have extensive, dependable metro systems. Using these metros to go about the cities is highly recommended. The metro systems are complemented by public buses and trams, which may transport you to locations not serviced by the subterranean network.

4. Taxis and Ride-sharing: In Spanish cities, taxis are widely accessible. It is customary to tip the taxi driver, so be sure the meter is functional. Or, in certain places, you may use ride-sharing services like Uber.

5. Bikes and scooters: Many Spanish towns have adopted bike- and scooter-sharing systems, making it simple and environmentally pleasant to explore metropolitan areas. The city should provide docks for scooters or bike stations.

6. Rental Cars: If you want to tour rural regions or smaller cities, hiring a vehicle could be a wise choice. The highway and road system of Spain is in good condition. On certain routes, there are tolls, so be aware of them and make sure you have the right insurance and permits.

7. Walking: One of the greatest ways to take in the beauty of Spain's cities and villages is to go for a stroll.

Walking distance separates many attractions, particularly in old city cores. You'll probably spend a lot of your exploration on foot, so wear comfortable shoes.

8. **Regional Transportation:** In addition to railroads, each area may provide a variety of other distinct modes of transportation. You may use the huge bus network in Andalusia, for instance, to tour the cities and villages there. You may be able to use funiculars and cable cars to ascend picturesque mountains in the Basque Country.

9. Language: It's a good idea to know a little bit of Spanish before visiting Spain since many people there may not speak English, particularly in the countryside. The enjoyment of your trip may be greatly increased by learning a few basic Spanish phrases.

10. **Transportation Cards:** You can buy transportation cards in many cities that give you savings on buses, trams, and metros. If you intend to use public transit regularly, these cards may be a cost-effective method of travel.

Overall, traveling to Spain for the first time may be a pleasant experience because of the country's well-developed transportation infrastructure and the variety of alternatives offered to visitors. Spain offers a transportation option to suit your requirements, whether you're visiting ancient towns, lounging on gorgeous beaches, or going on a hike through the breathtaking countryside.

Practical Steps To Stay Safe and healthy in Spain

The majority of the time, Spain is a safe place for tourists to visit, but like with any other place, it's important to exercise care.

To keep secure when traveling to Spain, follow these practical steps:

1. Study Your Destination properly: Before leaving on your vacation, do some study about the particular areas and towns you want to visit. It's important to be aware of the regional traditions, cultures, and safety issues.

2. Travel Insurance: Make sure you have complete travel insurance that covers unexpected medical expenses, trip cancellations, and theft or loss of personal possessions. Maintain emergency contact information and a copy of your insurance policy with you at all times.

3. Secure Your Belongings: Use a money belt or covert pouch to transport valuables like your passport, credit cards, and cash.

Store copies of your passport, identification card, and other crucial travel papers in a different location.

Store priceless goods in a hotel safe or locker.

Use ATMs only in safe, well-lit places and use caution while utilizing them.

4.Stay In Safe Accommodations: Consider your options carefully and check reviews from other tourists. Select accommodations in secure areas such as hotels and hostels.

Check that the safes and locks at your lodgings are secure so that your items are protected.

5. Avoid Pickpocketing: - Keep an eye out in busy areas like markets, public transit, and tourist sites.

Make use of anti-theft backpacks or bags with secret compartments and tight zippers.

Only bring what you need for the day; store valuables in your hotel safe.

6. Emergency Numbers: Become familiar with emergency contact numbers, such as 112, which is the universal emergency number in Europe.

Be aware of where the closest consulate or embassy for your nation is located.

7. Be Cautious in Popular Areas: Be aware of your surroundings, particularly in popular tourist areas.

Be on the lookout for distractions or people who could approach you and make odd demands.

Keep everything you own safe and in plain view.

8. Use Reliable Transportation: Pick trustworthy taxi services that are registered and accredited.

Be wary of pickpockets while utilizing public transit, particularly in packed metros and buses.

Get acquainted with the regional traffic regulations and road signs if you hire a vehicle.

9. Health Precautions: Check your immunization records and think about receiving the appropriate immunizations for Spain.

Consume bottled water or purify your water using water-purification techniques to prevent water-borne diseases.

Be careful while eating at street booths to keep your food clean.

10.   Respect   Local Customs:

Be aware of regional traditions and cultural standards.

When attending places of worship, wear modest clothing.

Steer clear of affectionate public shows in conservative neighborhoods.

11. Language Skills:

Acquire a few foundational Spanish expressions to make conversation easier, particularly in less-visited locales.

To help with language hurdles, take into account employing translation applications.

12. Stay Informed:

Keep Current on Local News and Any Safety Advisories for Your Destination.

To ensure your safety and the protection of other passengers, register with your embassy or consulate.

13. Socialize Wisely: Use care while mingling with strangers, particularly in regions with vibrant nightlife.

Refrain from taking food or beverages from total strangers.

If you decide to go on a trip, always choose trustworthy travel companies.

You may have a safe and pleasurable time while seeing the fascinating and beautiful nation of Spain if you adhere to these practical recommendations and have a general awareness of your surroundings.

Do's And Don'ts In Spain

It might be helpful to understand Spain's culture

and traditions by being aware of the dos and don'ts to ensure a courteous and pleasurable stay. Here are some essential rules to remember:

Do's:

1. Greet with Two Kisses: When greeting someone in Spain, it's usual to give them two kisses on each cheek, beginning with the left cheek. In more formal settings, a handshake is also appropriate.

2. Wear Modestly: Although dressing standards in Spain are typically permissive, it is appropriate to wear modestly when visiting places of worship, such as churches and cathedrals. In these settings, stay away from beachwear and exposed clothing.

3. Use Polite Language: Courtesy is highly valued in Spanish culture. Using the words "por favor" (please) and "gracias" (thank you) often will improve your communication skills. Unless you have been specifically asked to use their first name, address someone as "Mr." or "Seora," respectively.

4.   Enjoy   the Siesta: Numerous companies have a mid-afternoon break for the siesta, particularly in smaller cities and rural regions. Be prepared; at this period, several stores and eateries can be closed for a few hours.

5.   Respect   Meal Times: Meal times in Spain may be different from your own. The normal lunch hour is from 1:30 to 3:30, while the typical supper hour is from 8:30 to 10:00. Prepare yourself for later meals.

6.   Sample   the   local fare: Spanish food is delectable and unique. Be daring and sample regional cuisines like churros, paella, and tapas. A cost-effective option to experience local cuisine is to get a "menu del da" (menu of the day) at lunch.

7.   Keep   Cash Handy: Although   most places take credit cards, it's a good idea to have some cash on hand, particularly in smaller towns and for quick transactions.

8. Respect Quiet Hours: In residential neighborhoods, "siesta" hours may be observed in the afternoon, and there may be a general expectation that noise levels will be low in the evening. Be aware of any noise restrictions in your community.

Don'ts:

1.   Don't   Rush Mealtime: Meals   are supposed to be savored and appreciated in Spain. It is considered rude to eat quickly. Enjoy each meal slowly and thoroughly.

2.   Don't   Forget   to Tip: Even though service fees are often included in the bill, it's customary to leave a little tip, typically 10%.

Rounding up the bill is typical at cafés and bars.

3. Don't Expect English Everywhere: Even while many Spaniards, particularly in major cities, speak English in tourist areas, don't expect that everyone does. It might be quite beneficial to learn a few simple Spanish expressions.

4. Don't Raise Your Voice: It is considered impolite in Spain to speak loudly or yell in public. Keep your voice volume at a reasonable level, particularly in restaurants and on public transit.

5. Don't Interrupt Siesta: Some companies may shut during siesta hours, and residents may take a rest. In residential neighborhoods, refrain from creating a lot of noise or doing anything disturbing.

6. Paella is typically a lunchtime meal: so avoid ordering it at night. Since paella is often freshly made for lunch, ordering it at supper in Spain may not result in the greatest paella.

7. Don't Talk About Religion or Politics Casually: In Spain, these subjects might be touchy. Unless you are familiar with the individuals you are speaking to, avoid getting into heated debates over politics or religion.

Remember that etiquette and traditions in Spain might differ by location, so it's a good idea to investigate the place you want to visit to be aware of any unique aspects of the community. Respecting Spanish culture and traditions can improve your overall travel experience and promote amicable relationships with locals.

CHAPTER 4

Interesting Things To Do In Spain

There are a ton of exciting things to do in Spain because of its diverse culture, history, and stunning natural surroundings. Spain has much to offer no matter your interests—be they in history, gastronomy, art, or outdoor recreation. The following intriguing activities are worth taking into account while you're there:

1. Take a tour of the Alhambra in Granada. This magnificent palace and castle complex is a masterpiece of Islamic design and is included on the UNESCO World Heritage List. Its exquisite castles, gardens, and courtyards are open for exploration.

2. Visit La Sagrada Familia in Barcelona: This stunning church, an Antoni Gaud creation, is well-known for its distinctive architectural style. Don't miss the opportunity to see the inside and admire the magnificent stained glass windows.

3. Attend a Flamenco Show: Explore the fervor and ferocity of authentic Spanish Flamenco music and dance. Although there are Flamenco performances in numerous places, Seville is known for having a strong Flamenco tradition.

4. Enjoy Tapas: Spanish food is famed for its tapas, which are tiny, tasty appetizers that are served with beverages. Taste the regional delicacies of local tapas from different locations. Pintxos, a Basque Country-style tapas dish, is available in San Sebastián.

5. journey the Camino de Santiago: Set off on a long-distance journey or pilgrimage along the Camino de Santiago, a system of historic pilgrimage paths that leads to the Galician city of Santiago de Compostela. It provides a unique adventure in terms of culture and religion.

6. Explore one of the world's most renowned art institutions, the Prado Museum in Madrid, which has a sizable collection of European art, including pieces by Velázquez, Goya, and El Greco.

7. See Park Güell in Barcelona: The whimsical public park known as Park Güell, which has bright mosaics, sculptures, and architectural marvels, is another one of Antoni Gaud's works of art.

8. Unwind on Costa del Sol Beaches: Take in the splendor of southern Spain's Costa del Sol beaches. Three well-known coastal towns with favorable Mediterranean climates are Marbella, Malaga, and Nerja.

9. Pay a visit to Bilbao's Guggenheim
Museum: This famous museum, which Frank Gehry designed, is well known for its collection of modern art and cutting-edge design.
10. The White Villages (Pueblos Blancos) should be explored. White-washed towns built on slopes may be seen in Andalusia, a picturesque region. The most beautiful places to visit are Ronda, Grazalema, and Mijas.
11. Participate in the greatest food fight in history during the La Tomatina festival in Buol, where people toss tomatoes at one another in a friendly competition.
12. Wonder at the Córdoba Mosque-Cathedral: An unusual fusion of Islamic and Christian architecture may be seen in this old structure. It is an incredible piece of architecture that displays the city's rich past.
13. Ski in the Pyrenees: If you go to Spain in the

winter, the Pyrenees provide fantastic skiing options, particularly in Catalonia and Aragón.

14. Attend a Bullfight (Corrida): Take in a classic Spanish bullfight, but be advised that this activity is divisive and may not be appropriate for all visitors.

15. Explore Spain's well-known wine areas, such as La Rioja, and take wine-tasting tours to sample some of the greatest wines produced there.

These are just a handful of the many fascinating things to do in Spain. Diverse experiences are available for visitors with different interests thanks to the nation's diversity and rich cultural history.

Beaches to explore in Spain

Spain has a lengthy coastline along the Mediterranean Sea, Atlantic Ocean, and Bay of Biscay, which contributes to its reputation for having stunning beaches. Spain offers beaches to fit your interests, whether they are for unwinding, participating in water sports, or admiring the beautiful coastal environment. Here are a few of Spain's best beaches to visit:

1. Playa de la Concha in San Sebastián: This urban beach is often cited as one of the most exquisite urban beaches in all of Europe. Swimming and tanning are made easy by the bay's crescent shape, crystal-clear waters, and picturesque promenade.

2. Cala Comte, Ibiza: Cala Comte is a well-known beach on the island of Ibiza because of its clean seas and magnificent sunsets. The lively beach bars and snorkeling are both fantastic here.

3. Playa de Bolonia, Tarifa: This beach is well-known for its golden dunes and turquoise waves and is located on the Costa de la Luz. It's a less congested alternative to some of the busier beaches in southern Spain.

4. The Beach of the Cathedrals in Galicia, sometimes called Playa de las Catedrales, is a distinctive beach with beautiful rock formations that resemble cathedral arches. You should go there at low tide so you may explore the natural "cathedrals."

5. Playa de Ses Illetes, Formentera: This beach, which is located on the little island of Formentera, is sometimes likened to the Caribbean because of its immaculate white beaches and shallow, clear water. Swimmers and sunbathers will find it to be a heaven.

6. Playa de la Victoria in Cadiz is renowned for its energetic vibe, water sports, and beachfront bars. It's a terrific location for both enjoying the sun and Andalusian food.

7. Playa de Maspalomas, Gran Canaria: With its

enormous dunes that reach the sea, Maspalomas provides a distinctive environment. It's a well-liked location for camel rides and windsurfing.

8. Playa de Papagayo, Lanzarote: These hidden coves on the island of Lanzarote are renowned for their crystal-clear seas and volcanic surroundings. Hiking and snorkeling are also excellent in the region.

9. Playa de Rodas, Ces Islands: This beach, which is a part of the Galician coast and is located in the Ces Islands, is renowned for its unspoiled beauty, hiking paths, and protected habitat. To protect the environment, access is restricted.

10. Playa de la Malagueta, Malaga: This urban beach in Malaga provides a combination of leisure activities and cultural sights. It is ideal for visitors since it is near to the city core.

11. Playa de La Barrosa, Chiclana de la Frontera: Located on the

Costa de la Luz, this family-friendly beach has superb golden sands and a boardwalk dotted with eateries and stores.

12. Playa de Palma, Mallorca: This beach on the island of Mallorca is well-known for its exciting nightlife. Both enjoyment and relaxation are well suited to it.

These are just a few of Spain's breathtaking beaches. There are many more. From Barcelona's vibrant metropolitan beaches to the peaceful coves of the Balearic Islands, each locale has its distinct charm to offer. Spain's coastlines offer something for everyone, whether you're looking for excitement or tranquility.

Historical Sites In Spain

There are many historical sites in Spain, many of which have had a significant impact on the development of European and global history. Spain has a long and diversified past, which is represented in its many historical sites. The historical eras, cultures, and civilizations represented at these places provide a fascinating look into Spain's history. Here is a quick summary of some of Spain's most well-known historical sites:

1. The Alhambra: is One of the most famous historical landmarks in Spain in Granada, which is a marvel of Islamic construction. It was first built as a palace and stronghold for Muslim emperors in the middle of the 13th century under the Nasrid Dynasty. The elaborate palaces, courtyards, and gardens serve as a living museum for the creative and cultural accomplishments of Andalusian Islamic civilization.

2. The Sagrada Familia in Barcelona: This basilica, which is currently being built but was created by famous architect Antoni Gaud, is a representation of Catalonia's creative and architectural legacy. It is anticipated that the work, which started in 1882, will be finished soon. Incorporating elements of Gothic and Art Nouveau, it has a distinctive modernist design.

3. Alcázar of Seville: The Alcázar of Seville, a magnificent royal palace, was first built as a stronghold in the tenth century. It displays a variety of architectural designs, including Islamic, Gothic, Renaissance, and Mudejar styles. Many monarchs, including Christian kings and Moorish caliphs, have lived at the palace.

4. The Aqueduct of Segovia: Constructed in the first century AD, the Roman Aqueduct of Segovia is a feat of engineering. It is 818 meters in length and is made of almost 25,000 granite pieces that were put together without the use of mortar.

Over several centuries, this aqueduct delivered water to the city.

5. The Mezquita Cathedral in Cordoba is a unique building that serves as a representation of the changes in Spain's religion and culture. It was a Visigothic church at first, then during Islamic dominion it was turned into a mosque, and finally it was turned into a Catholic cathedral. A captivating forest of columns and arches can be seen throughout the interior.

6. The Great Mosque of Toledo: which was constructed in the 10th century during the rule of the Umayyad Caliph Al-Hakam II, is a magnificent example of Islamic architecture. Later, it was transformed into a cathedral, illuminating the confluence of Islamic and Christian civilizations in medieval Spain.

7. Roman Theatre of Mérida: This remarkably well-preserved Roman theater, built in the first century BC, provides evidence of the Roman presence in Spain. Currently still in service, it has a seating capacity of nearly 6,000.

8. Altamira Cave: Situated in northern Spain, Altamira Cave is well known for its Upper Paleolithic era, or around 36,000-year-old, ancient cave paintings. These extraordinary artworks include animal depictions and provide light on early humans' creative prowess.

9. The huge church and memorial known as the "Valley of the Fallen " (Valle de los Casos), which was constructed during the Franco era and is located close to Madrid, is cut into the hillside. Because of its connection to Spain's fascist history, the location—which houses General Francisco Franco's tomb—is contentious.

These historical locations in Spain take visitors on an enthralling trip through time while demonstrating the intricate history of the nation and the effects of many civilizations. Through them, tourists may discover the architectural, artistic, and cultural accomplishments of Spain's rich legacy and feel a direct link to the past.

Top Museums and galleries in Spain

Innumerable top-notch museums and galleries with a wide variety of art, history, and culture can be found across Spain. These institutions provide an enthralling tour through the nation's rich legacy and the contributions made by Spanish artists across the world. Some of Spain's best museums and galleries are listed below:

1. The Museo del Prado in Madrid: The Prado Museum, which is often ranked among the top art galleries in the world, has a sizable collection of European works. It includes paintings by painters including Titian, Rubens, and Hieronymus Bosch with Spanish masters like Velázquez and Goya.

2. Museo Reina Sofia, Madrid: This institution for contemporary art is well-known for hosting Pablo Picasso's enduring masterpiece, "Guernica." Additionally, the Reina Sofia exhibits works by notable foreign painters like Georges Braque and Francis Bacon as well as other well-known Spanish artists like Salvador Dali and Joan Miró.

3. Museo Guggenheim Bilbao: This modern art gallery was created by Frank Gehry and is renowned for both its architectural inventiveness and its art collection. There are pieces by Jeff Koons, Andy Warhol, and Richard Serra among others.

4. Museo Picasso, Barcelona: This museum is host to one of the largest collections of Pablo Picasso's paintings from the

20th century. It is situated in the center of Barcelona's old Gothic Quarter. It gives information on the creative development of the artist.

5. The Thyssen-Bornemisza Museum in Madrid: This institution is home to a substantial private collection of European artwork spanning many centuries. The Italian Renaissance, Dutch Baroque, Impressionism, and other artistic movements are represented, as well as works by Van Gogh, Dürer, and Hopper.

6. Museo Nacional Centro de Arte Reina Sofia, Madrid: In addition to "Guernica," this museum is home to an outstanding collection of modern and contemporary art. Artists including Julio González, Juan Gris, and Joan Miró have pieces in it.

7. El Prado Museum: located in Madrid's Buen Retiro Park, is another outstanding gallery devoted to ornamental arts. From the Romanesque era to the nineteenth century, it has a substantial collection of European paintings, sculptures, and decorative arts.

8. MNAC in Barcelona, the "Museu Nacional d'Art de Catalunya": The MNAC, located atop Montjuic Hill, is renowned for its outstanding collection of Catalan artwork, which includes Romanesque paintings, Gothic altarpieces, and Modernist masterpieces. One of the highlights is the museum's panoramic vista.

9. The Salvador Dali Theatre Museum in Figueres: This museum was designed by Dali himself and offers a strange experience. It has a sizable collection of the artist's creations, giving access to his unique and innovative mind.

10. Reales Alcázares, Seville: Although not a typical museum, Seville's Royal Alcazar is a magnificent palace complex with a significant architectural heritage. It is renowned for its sophisticated use of Gothic, Baroque, Mudejar, and Renaissance architectural styles.

These renowned Spanish museums and galleries are cultural gems that provide visitors a chance to fully immerse themselves in the nation's creative and historical heritage.

Parks And Gardens In Spain

Some of Spain's most well-known parks and gardens are listed below:

Generalife Gardens in Granadilla: One of Spain's most exquisite gardens is the Generalife Gardens, which is a UNESCO World Heritage Site. The Nasrid dynasty constructed the gardens, which are a great example of Moorish architecture and design. They were constructed in the 13th century.

Parque del Retiro in Madrid
The biggest and most well-known park in Madrid is Parque del Retiro. A lake, gardens, an Alfonso XII monument, and the Crystal Palace are just a few of the park's many attractions.

1. The Alhambra Gardens in Granada: Granada's Alhambra palace complex has many gardens collectively known as the Jardines de la Alhambra. The gardens are well-known for their lovely flowers, fountains, and cityscape vistas.

2. Jardines de la Casa de Pilatos In Seville: A collection of gardens known as the Jardines de la Casa de Pilatos is housed within the Casa de Pilatos castle in Seville. The gardens are renowned for its gorgeous orange trees, fountains, and Mudéjar architecture.

3. Málaga Jardines de la Concepción: A botanical park called the Jardines de la Concepción in Málaga. A vast range of international plants and flowers may be found in the garden.

4. Gardens of the Palau Güell in Barcelona: The Jardines del Palau Güell is a collection of gardens within Barcelona's Palau Güell palace. The gardens, whose distinctive and quirky design was the work of Antoni Gaud, are well-known.

5. The Barcelona Park, Parc de la Ciutadella: A sizable park called Parc de la Ciutadella is situated in Barcelona. The park contains several attractions, such as a zoo, a museum, a lake, and other gardens.

6. Park de Maria Luisa in Seville: Seville is home to the sizable park known as Parque de maria Luisa. There are several different attractions in the park, including a lake, gardens, a statue of Christopher Columbus, and the Plaza de Espana.

7. Parc de la Turia in Valencia: A sizable park called Parque de la Turia is situated in Valencia. The

Turia River's previous riverbed served as the foundation for the construction of the park, which offers several amenities including gardens, a bike path, and several other recreational areas.

8. Javieres de Sabatini, Madrid: The grounds known as the Jardines de Sabatini may be found behind Madrid's Royal Palace. Known for their stunning fountains, sculptures, and vistas of the palace, the gardens were created in the 18th century.

In Madrid, the Jardines del Campo del Moro, The Jardines del Campo del Moro are a collection of gardens near to Madrid's Royal Palace. The gardens, which are currently accessible to the general public, were formerly the royal family of Spain's hunting grounds.

9. Gardens of the Alcázar, Seville: Within Seville's Alcázar palace are many gardens known as the

Jardines del Alcázar. The Moorish kingdom constructed the gardens in the 12th century, and they are renowned for their lovely fountains, flowers, and orange trees.

These are just a handful of the stunning parks and gardens Spain has to offer.

Shopping in Spain

Shopping in Spain: A Tale of Contrasts between Luxurious and Inexpensive Stores,

Spain has plenty to offer for every taste and price range, whether you're an experienced traveler searching for premium brands or a frugal shopper seeking out one-of-a-kind bargains.

The height of elegance is found in luxury shopping.

Some of the most well-known designers and premium fashion businesses in the world have their roots in Spain. Several cities stand out when it comes to luxury shopping, including:

1. **Madrid:** The Spanish capital is a hotspot for upscale shopping. Designer shops and luxury department stores like El Corte Inglés are particularly well known in the Salamanca neighborhood. You can discover renowned worldwide names like Chanel, Louis Vuitton, and Gucci as well as famous Spanish brands like Loewe, Balenciaga, and Manolo Blahnik here.

2. Barcelona: The best spot to go for upscale shopping in Barcelona is Passeig de Gràcia. Prestigious retailers including Prada, Dolce & Gabbana, and Versace have flagship locations along this street. The posh El Triangle shopping area and the shops in the Eixample neighborhood are other attractions of the city.

3. **Marbella:** Marbella, located on the glitzy Costa del Sol, has a special mix of opulent shops, posh malls, and expensive jewelry stores. Particularly well-known for its upscale shopping experiences is the Puerto Banus region.

4. Ibiza: Popular for its thriving nightlife, Ibiza also attracts high-end shopping. There are businesses on the island that offer designer beachwear and accessories, ideal for the upscale beachgoer.

It's crucial to keep an eye on your budget even if luxury shopping in Spain is a lovely experience. High-end fashion products may be expensive, therefore it's a good idea to establish a spending limit to prevent overspending.

Low-cost Shopping: Discover Hidden Treasures
Markets and neighborhood stores in Spain offer thrifty buyers fantastic chances to get one-of-a-kind goods without breaking the bank. Here are a few inexpensive shopping opportunities to enjoy:

1.   Local marketplaces: Spain's marketplaces are a veritable gold mine of reasonably priced treasures. From Barcelona's thriving Mercat de Sant Josep de la Boqueria to Madrid's El Rastro flea market, you may shop a variety of products, including apparel, accessories, antiques, and crafts. Never forget to barter for the greatest prices!

2. Thrift Stores (Ropa de Segunda   Mano): Thrift shops are becoming more and more well-liked in Spain since they provide used apparel and accessories at reasonable costs. These stores offer buyers unique antique goods and eco-friendly shopping options.

3.   Spanish   Fashion Chains: Several reasonably priced fashion chains, like Zara, Mango, and Pull & Bear, are found in Spain. These companies provide affordable, stylish apparel and accessories. *They have* *shops in practically every town and city.*

4. Souvenirs and Local Crafts: Spain is well known for its handmade goods. Visit regional markets and stores to find handmade pottery, leather products, jewelry, and traditional Spanish fans while you are in places like Toledo, Granada, or Seville.

5. Discount Stores: Stores selling famous brands and designer products from the previous season are dispersed across Spain. Two well-known outlet malls are located between Madrid and Barcelona: Las Rozas Village and La Roca Village.

6.Supermarkets and Department shops: Spanish grocers like Mercadona and department shops like Primark provide reasonably priced apparel and home goods. These shops are great for picking your daily necessities.

7. Discount Shopping Events: Keep an eye out for seasonal deals and events like the "Rebajas" (sales) that happen in Spain, particularly between January and July. During certain times, you may get fantastic prices on apparel, footwear, and accessories.

While low-cost shopping in Spain may be a great opportunity to locate one-of-a-kind things and souvenirs, the quality might vary. Before making a purchase, be sure to give each item a thorough inspection and weigh its worth.

Luxury and inexpensive shopping coexist together in Spain, providing visitors with a diverse retail experience. Shopping in Spain is a pleasant trip where you may discover both the luxurious and the reasonably priced.

Events and festivals in Spain

Spain is renowned for having a wide variety of lively festivals and events that often highlight the rich customs, cultural legacy, and creative spirit of its many areas. Here are some important holidays and events that have occurred in Spain, along with a sneak peek at what to anticipate:

1. La Tomatina in Bunol, Valencia:

La Tomatina is the biggest food battle in the world, taking place on the last Wednesday of August. Participants hurl ripe tomatoes at one another in Bunol's streets. Thousands of visitors flock to this fun and chaotic event.

Participate in the mayhem by getting into a friendly tomato battle with both residents and visitors. If you don't mind being coated with tomato pulp, wear old clothing.

2. Feria de Abril in Seville:
Two weeks after Easter.

With flamenco dance, bullfights, horse displays, and colorful casitas (decorated tents), this traditional Andalusian fair honors the local way of life.

Enjoy mouthwatering Andalusian food, energetic flamenco dancing, and seeing Sevillanas dancers spin in vibrant costumes.

3. San Fermán (Pamplona): July 6 to July 14, San Fermán is well-known for its running of the bulls, a dangerous event when brave competitors sprint through the streets in front of charging bulls. The week also includes celebrations, parades, and religious occasions.

Take part in the experience by running with the bulls or watching from a safe distance. Join the fun street gatherings where traditional cuisine and sangria are served.

4. Tenerife's Santa Cruz of Tenerife Carnival

February or March (depending on when Easter falls).

The Carnival of Santa Cruz is one of the biggest and most vibrant carnivals in the world, with ornate costumes, parades, and music.

Don gaudy garb and watch the parades, which include magnificent floats and dancing groups. Don't forget to attend the carnival queen's coronation.

5.   La   Mercè (Barcelona): La Mercè, the city's biggest street celebration, honors the patron saint of the city and is held on September 24. Various cultural activities are presented there, such as concerts and customary parades.

Take in the spectacle of the Castells (human tower) contests, the Correfoc (fire run) featuring fire-breathing dragons, and the captivating street entertainment.

6.   Las   Fallas (Valencia): This festival is a burst of art, fire, and music. It takes place from March 15 to March 19. The event concludes with a dramatic burning of the enormous, satirical sculptures (fallas) that are on display across the city.

Discover the streets to marvel at the elaborate fallas and take in the nighttime fireworks displays. Observe the magnificent "Nit del Foc" (Night of Fire) performance.

7. Festival of Patios (Cordoba)

Early May is the time of this UNESCO-listed festival, which highlights Cordoba's stunning patios (courtyards), which are festooned with vibrant flowers. For the most exquisitely adorned patio, there is a competition.

Visit private patios that are often off-limits to the public and take in the talent and hard work that homeowners put into producing these gorgeous flower arrangements.

8. Caravaca de la Cruz, or the Running of the Wine Horses, takes place on May 2.

This unusual celebration features horse races pulling wine barrels through the streets of the town. It takes place during the town's religious events.

Enjoy the celebrations while taking in the thrilling races, the ornately decorated horses, and local wines.

These celebrations and events in Spain provide a window into the vibrant culture, long traditions, and enthusiasm for life of the nation. Whether you're looking for the thrill of running with the bulls or the beauty of flower patios, Spain's festivals offer remarkable experiences that honor its different regions and thriving communities.

Spain's nightlife

Spain has a thriving nightlife that is infused with rich culture, bright energy, and a strong respect for the art of enjoying life when the sun goes down. It's a compelling place where residents and tourists go to enjoy the beauty of the night and make lifelong memories.

The streets of Spain come alive with an undeniable attraction as day turns into night. Open-air events may be held on charming terraces and plazas thanks to the pleasant Mediterranean environment. The enticing smells of Spanish food, music, and laughing fill the air at night.

The tapas crawl is one of the most typical experiences in Spain. You may discover tapas bars that serve a great selection of little, savory foods in towns like Barcelona, Madrid, and Seville. Each taste, from the scrumptious jamón ibérico to the crunchy patatas bravas, is a flavor explosion that goes well with a drink of sangria or regional wine. The feeling of community that results from sharing these delicious sweets with friends or new acquaintances is unique to Spain's nightlife.

The Spanish nightlife is not complete without live music. Flamenco performances might be stumbled upon in small-scale settings, while live jazz, salsa, and techno music can be heard in buzzing bars. Whether you're a seasoned dancer or merely sway to the music, the rhythmic rhythms, and passionate songs will have you moving to the music and dancing the night away.

Beyond the cuisine and music, Spain's nightlife is beautiful because of the people you encounter. Since locals are renowned for their friendliness and openness, chatting with a Spaniard or other visitor is simple. A spirit of friendship develops as tales, jokes, and experiences are shared beneath the starry Spanish sky, making every night out memorable.

The streets transform into a living mural as night falls, with vibrant lights lighting grand mansions and busy squares. Simply said, the atmosphere is magical. The atmosphere is nothing short of beautiful, whether you're strolling through the cobblestone streets of Granada or the tiny lanes of Barcelona's Gothic Quarter.

The people of Spain create a picture of beauty, connection, and amazing experiences on the canvas of the night. You will fall in love with Spain's nightlife and desire to go back again and again after you've experienced its charming and lovely spirit.

CHAPTER 5

Top 15 hotels in Spain

Certainly, the following is a basic rundown of some of Spain's best hotels:

1. The Ritz-Carlton, Madrid, first: This historic hotel provides traditional grandeur and elegance and is located in the center of Madrid. It is a symbol of affluent life because of its lavish décor, Michelin-starred cuisine, and famed afternoon tea.

2. Mandarin Oriental Ritz, Madrid: It has been restored and renamed as a Mandarin Oriental property after being The Ritz Madrid. In addition to opulent lodging, top-notch cuisine, and a tranquil garden patio, it nonetheless has a timeless charm.

3. Hotel Arts Barcelona: This modern hotel, located on Barcelona's waterfront, offers magnificent sea views, opulent accommodations, and a noteworthy art collection. Enoteca, a restaurant with a Michelin star, is well renowned.

4. El Palace Barcelona: El Palace, a landmark in Barcelona, combines a classic appeal with contemporary amenities. The hotel offers gourmet food at the Caelis restaurant, a rooftop pool, and a stunning design.

5. The Serras Hotel in Barcelona: A premier position along Barcelona's seafront is offered by this boutique hotel. With a rooftop pool, Michelin-starred restaurants, and stunning vistas, it combines contemporary architecture with a historic front.

6. The Finca Cortesin Hotel, Golf & Spa: This opulent resort, which can be found on the Costa del Sol, blends Andalusian and Moorish design. It is well known for its world-class golf course, Kabuki Raw restaurant, and opulent spa.

7. Hotel Alfonso XIII: The following are some details of the Hotel Alfonso XIII, a Luxury Collection Hotel, in Seville: This Seville landmark hotel has exquisite Andalusian architecture. A real jewel in the city, it has opulent rooms, lovely gardens, and a classic Spanish patio.

8. Gran Hotel Inglés: This boutique hotel, which is located in Madrid, is renowned for its Art Deco style and upscale atmosphere. It is close to the city's attractions and has a chic cocktail bar.

9. Hacienda Na Xamena in Ibiza: This Ibiza hotel, perched on a cliff with a view of the Mediterranean, provides stunning scenery and a tranquil setting. With its infinity pools, spa, and private patios, it's the ideal getaway.

10. The Hotel Villa Magna in Madrid: This opulent hotel in Salamanca, a posh area of Madrid, offers spacious accommodations, superb cuisine at the Magnum Bar & Restaurant, and a tranquil courtyard garden.

11. Hotel Santo Mauro, Madrid, Autograph Collection: A feeling of grandeur permeates this Madrid boutique hotel that was formerly a neoclassical palace. The Santo Mauro Restaurant, a lovely garden, and magnificent accommodations are all present.

12. Hotel Urban:, a Luxury Collection Hotel in Madrid

This modern hotel is conveniently located among Madrid's biggest attractions and has an avant-garde design, a rooftop patio with a pool, and the Glass Mar restaurant serving Mediterranean cuisine.

13. The Westin Palace, Madrid: This large hotel is a historical treasure in the center of Madrid and offers elaborate design, roomy accommodations, and dining at La Rotonda. For more than a century, dignitaries and celebrities have enjoyed it.

14. Gran Hotel Miramar GL: Barcelona This opulent hotel, which is oceanfront in Barcelona, provides opulent lodging, rooms with views of the ocean, and great cuisine at the Prêt-à-Portea restaurant.

14. Hotel Arts Barcelona: As was already said, this chic, modern hotel is situated on the waterfront of Barcelona and offers spectacular views, a sumptuous spa, and modern amenities.

Whether you want modern luxury, calm seaside leisure, or traditional elegance, these hotels in Spain can accommodate a variety of tastes and preferences. Travelers looking for the finest in hospitality may choose from any of them for a distinctive and unforgettable experience.

Camping In Spain

From verdant woods to unspoiled beaches and rocky mountains, Spain is home to many beautiful camping locations. Here's a look at the Spanish camping scene:

1. Diverse Landscapes: Spain's varied topography offers a variety of camping alternatives. Spain offers it all, whether you're looking for the peace of Pyrenean woodlands, the seaside splendor of Costa Brava, the dramatic scenery of the Sierra Nevada, or the deserts of Almera.

2. Natural areas and parks in the United States: Spain is a great destination for those who love the outdoors since it has so many national parks and natural areas. Parks where you may camp in unspoiled wilderness include Ordesa y Monte Perdido National Park, Picos de Europa, and Doana National Park.

3. Beach Camping: Spain's lengthy coastline provides a plethora of options for beach camping. You may pitch your tent only feet from the ocean at Andalusia's Costa de la Luz or Valencia's Costa Blanca. In the Balearic Islands and Catalonia's Costa Brava, beach camping is especially well-liked.

4. Camino de Santiago: The Camino de Santiago is a well-known pilgrimage path that annually draws thousands of walkers and campers. It is a unique camping experience with cultural and spiritual importance since there are designated campsites and hostels along the road where you may stay on a budget.

5.   campsites   and Amenities: Spain has a well-established network of campsites (campings) with amenities including showers, restrooms, electrical hookups, and social spaces. For those who would like a little more luxury, several campgrounds provide rental amenities like bungalows and cottages.

6.   Wild   camping   is permitted: in certain areas, like the Picos de Europa and sections of Catalonia, even though it is legally prohibited in many others. For a courteous and responsible camping experience, be sure to always check local laws and request permission when required.

7.   Adventure Activities: Adventure activities like hiking, mountain biking, kayaking, and rock climbing are often available when camping in Spain. Particularly in the Pyrenees, wonderful camping adventures are available.

8. Stargazing: Spain is a great place to go because of its pristine sky and minimal levels of light pollution. Consider camping in regions with clear skies, such as the Sierra Morena or the Canary Island of La Palma.

9. Cultural Experiences: Camping in Spain offers a great chance to get in touch with the local way of life. You may take part in festivals, eat native food, and socialize with welcoming people who could tell you about their customs over a campfire.

Check the particular rules and criteria of the area you want to visit before starting your camping trip in Spain. To guarantee an enjoyable and sustainable camping experience in this stunning nation, respect for the environment, regional traditions, and environmental conservation initiatives is vital.

CHAPTER 6

Top 10 luxury hotels in Spain

There are many luxurious hotels in Spain to select from, with options for every price range and taste. According to ratings and reviews from past visitors, these are the top 10 luxury hotels in Spain:

1. Spanish capital's Mandarin Oriental Ritz

A magnificent hotel in the center of the city is called the Mandarin Oriental Ritz, Madrid. It represents the height of grandeur and sophistication and has been welcoming visitors since 1910. The hotel includes 100 rooms and suites, all of which are well-furnished and equipped with contemporary conveniences. A wide range of top-notch eateries and bars are also available at The Mandarin Oriental Ritz, Madrid, including the Michelin-starred El Retiro restaurant.

2. The Ritz-Carlton, Madrid

Another famous hotel in the city center is The Ritz Madrid. The hotel is renowned for its opulent lodgings, top-notch cuisine, and breathtaking city views. The hotel includes 132 rooms and suites, all of which are exquisitely furnished and are equipped with contemporary conveniences. There are several top-notch dining establishments and bars at The Ritz Madrid, including the Michelin-starred Palm Court restaurant.

3. The Hotel Arts Barcelona

A modern hotel with amazing views of the Mediterranean Sea, the Hotel Arts Barcelona is situated directly on the beach. Celebrities and business travelers both prefer to use it. The hotel includes 483 rooms and suites, each of which is tastefully furnished and equipped with contemporary conveniences. The Michelin-starred Enoteca restaurant is among the several top-notch restaurants and bars that can be found at the Hotel Arts Barcelona.

4. El Palace Barcelona

The ancient hotel El Palace Barcelona is situated in the center of Barcelona. It delivers an opulent and sophisticated experience. There are 549 rooms and suites in the hotel, each of which is well-furnished and equipped with contemporary facilities. There are several top-notch eateries and bars at El Palace Barcelona, including the Michelin-starred Caelis restaurant.

5. The Serras Hotel Barcelona:

A restored 19th-century mansion now houses the boutique hotel The Serras Hotel Barcelona. It provides upscale lodgings and individualized service. The hotel includes 28 rooms and suites, all of which are well-furnished and equipped with contemporary conveniences. Dos Palillos, a restaurant in the Serras Hotel Barcelona, also has a Michelin star.

6. Hotel, golf, and spa Finca Cortesin:

A resort hotel may be found in the Andalusian countryside at Finca Cortesin Hotel, Golf & Spa. Luxurious lodgings, a top-notch golf course, and a cutting-edge spa are all available. The hotel includes 167 elegantly furnished rooms and suites, all of which are equipped with contemporary conveniences. There are several top-notch restaurants and bars at Finca Cortesin Hotel, Golf & Spa.

7. Seville's Hotel Alfonso XIII: a Luxury Collection Hotel.

In the center of Seville, there is a historic hotel called Hotel Alfonso XIII, a Luxury Collection Hotel.

Celebrities and business travelers both prefer to use it. The hotel includes 151 rooms and suites, each of which is well-furnished and equipped with contemporary conveniences. Seville's Hotel Alfonso XIII, a Luxury Collection Hotel, is home to several top-notch eateries and bars, including the Michelin-starred San Fernando.

8. Gran Hotel Inglés:

A five-star hotel called Gran Hotel Inglés is situated in the center of Madrid. Elegant lodging, top-notch cuisine, and breathtaking city views are all available here. The hotel includes 48 rooms and suites, all of which are well-furnished and equipped with contemporary conveniences. The Table by, a restaurant in Gran Hotel Inglés, also has a Michelin star.

9. Ibiza's Hacienda Na Xamena:

On a cliffside overlooking the Mediterranean Sea lies the opulent resort hotel known as Hacienda Na

Xamena. It provides various spa services and wellness programs in addition to breathtaking views of the coastline. The hotel includes 78 elegantly furnished rooms and suites, all of which are equipped with contemporary conveniences. Several top-notch restaurants and bars may be found in Hacienda Na Xamena.

10. Hotel Villa Magna, Madrid:

In the center of Madrid stands the five-star Hotel Villa Magna. It provides first-rate cuisine, opulent lodging, and breathtaking city vistas. The hotel includes 150 rooms and suites, all of which are well-furnished and equipped with contemporary conveniences. Tse Yang, another restaurant in Hotel Villa Magna, is Michelin-starred.

Whatever your needs or budget, Spain has the perfect luxury hotel for you. With so many wonderful options to pick from, you're sure to have a memorable and enjoyable visit.

Low budget hotels in Spain

Hostels, guesthouses, and low-cost hotels are just a few of the affordable lodging alternatives available in Spain. Here are a few cheap hotels you may find in various Spanish cities:

1. Barcelona's Hostal Orleans:
Affordably priced, clean, and pleasant rooms are available at this centrally situated guesthouse in Barcelona. For vacationers on a low budget, it's a fantastic choice.

2. TOC Hostel Madrid (Madrid): TOC Hostel in Madrid offers budget-conscious tourists chic and reasonably priced lodging. It offers both private rooms and dormitory-style accommodations, as well as a buzzing environment and social activities.

3. Sant Jordi Hostels Sagrada Familia in Barcelona: This hostel provides a lively environment, cozy dormitories, and reasonably priced private rooms and is close to the famous Sagrada Familia. For young and backpacking travelers, it's perfect.

4. Pensión Antonio (Seville): Simple, spotless rooms are available at reasonable prices at this beautiful Seville inn. Significant landmarks like the Seville Cathedral and Alcazar are conveniently close by.

5. Catalonia Park Güell, located in Barcelona: This inexpensive hotel, which is located in the Gràcia neighborhood, has cozy rooms and a rooftop terrace with expansive city views. The price is quite reasonable.

6. Pensión Miami (Madrid) Pensión Miami: a hotel in the center of Madrid, provides inexpensive lodging in simple yet tidy and pleasant rooms. Many sights are accessible by foot.

7. Hostal San Juan, in Granada: In Granada, this family-run inn offers reasonably priced lodging in a welcoming setting. Other historical landmarks, such as the Alhambra, are nearby.

8. Hotel Sancho

Budget-friendly lodging with contemporary conveniences is available at Valencia's Hotel Sancho. The City of Arts and Sciences is conveniently close by.

10. Hostal San Vicente II (Seville): This inexpensive Seville guesthouse provides simple, clean rooms at reasonable prices. The main attractions of the city are close by.

11. Hostal Adis (Madrid): In Madrid's Lavapiés area, Hostal Adis offers basic and inexpensive lodging. For vacationers on a tight budget, it's a fantastic option.

For those looking to see Spain on a budget, these

cost-effective hotels and guesthouses across the nation provide a cozy and affordable choice. The clean, modest conveniences they give let you conserve your money for seeing Spain's culture, food, and tourist sites.

Top 14 Restaurants In Spain

Spain is a nation with a long culinary history, and its restaurants provide a broad range of cuisines, including both classic Spanish food and cutting-edge, contemporary delicacies. The top 15 restaurants in Spain are listed below:

1. **Asador Etxebarri and Axpe:** This restaurant has received a Michelin star and is renowned for its use of fresh, seasonal ingredients and wood-fired cookery. Although the menu is always changing, you can

anticipate finding items such as grilled seafood, meats, and veggies.

2. **Girona's El Celler de Can Roca:** One of the most renowned restaurants in the world, this one has three Michelin stars. The restaurant's owners, the Roca brothers, are renowned for their inventive and artistic cuisine. Despite the menu's constant modifications, you can anticipate finding delicacies like pigeon with foie gras and black truffle as well as sea urchin with caviar and almond milk.

3. **Distinction, Barcelona:** This two-Michelin-star establishment is renowned for its cutting-edge cooking techniques and use of molecular

gastronomy.
Although the menu is always changing, you can expect to discover items like edible helium-filled balloons and liquid olives.

4. **Mugaritz and Errenteria:** The inventive and adventurous food of this two-Michelin-starred establishment is renowned. Although the menu is always changing, you can anticipate seeing meals like edible earth and edible wood.

5. **DiverXO en Madrid:** This three-Michelin-star establishment is renowned for its inventive and amusing food. The menu changes constantly, but you can count on seeing items like lobster with caviar and lemon and

liquid egg with foie gras and truffle.

6. **Quique Dacosta and Denia:** This three-Michelin-star establishment is renowned for its seafood specialties and inventive cooking methods. Although the menu is always changing, you can anticipate finding meals like sea urchin with caviar and lemon and red mullet with smoked eel and avocado.

7. **El Puerto de Santa Maria, Aponiente**: The seafood dishes served at this two-Michelin-star establishment are well-known, as are the creative cooking methods used. Although the menu is always changing, you can count on finding items like sea urchin with caviar and lemon

and tuna with caviar and lemon.

8. **Martin Berasategui and Lasarte-Oria:** The traditional Basque cuisine served at this three-Michelin-star establishment is renowned for its use of seasonal, fresh ingredients. Although the menu is always changing, you can anticipate finding items such as grilled seafood, meats, and veggies.

9. **Abac, Barcelona:** The food of this three-Michelin-star establishment is renowned for its creativity and innovation. Although the menu is always changing, you can count on finding items like pigeon with foie gras and black truffle as well as foie gras with truffle and hazelnut.

10. **Barcelona's Lasarte:** The traditional Basque cuisine served at this two-Michelin-star establishment is renowned for its use of seasonal, fresh ingredients. Although the menu is always changing, you can anticipate finding items such as grilled seafood, meats, and veggies.

11. **San Sebastian's Akelarre:** This three-Michelin-star establishment is renowned for its seafood specialties and inventive cooking methods. Although the menu is always changing, you can anticipate finding meals like sea urchin with caviar and lemon and red mullet with smoked eel and avocado.

12. **San Sebastián's Arzak:** One of the most renowned

restaurants in the world, this one has three Michelin stars. The restaurant's owners, the Arzak family, are renowned for their inventive and artistic fare. Although the menu is always changing, you can anticipate finding meals like pigeon with foie gras and black truffle as well as sea urchin with caviar and lemon.

13. **Nerua and Bilbao:** The Basque cuisine served at this one-Michelin-star establishment is renowned, as is the use of local, fresh ingredients. Although the menu is always changing, you can anticipate finding items such as grilled seafood, meats, and veggies.

14. **Madrid's La Terraza del Casino:** This one-

Michelin-star establishment is renowned for its traditional Spanish cooking and seasonal use of fresh ingredients. Although the menu is always changing, you can anticipate finding items such as grilled seafood, meats, and veggies.

15. **Azurmendi and Larrabetzu:** The food of this three-Michelin-star establishment is renowned for its creativity and innovation. Although the menu is always changing, you can anticipate finding meals like pigeon with foie gras and black truffle as well as sea urchin with caviar and lemon.

These are just a handful of Spain's many excellent restaurants. You're sure to locate the ideal location to have a delectable lunch with so many selections to choose from.

Coffee Shops And Cafes

The tradition of café with leche (coffee with milk) and various coffee variants is strongly ingrained in everyday life in Spain, where people take their coffee seriously. Here are some locations in Spain where you may sip on a delicious cup of coffee:

1. Cafeteras: Cafeteras are the standard example of a coffee establishment in Spain. These places often open early in the morning and provide breakfast fare including tostadas (toasted bread with tomato and olive oil), freshly made coffee, and pastries. The best places to have a fast café solo (single espresso) or a leisurely café con leche are cafeterias.

2. Bares: In Spain, bars provide more than just

alcoholic beverages; they also provide coffee service. You are free to order your chosen coffee type, whether it be a plain café americano (diluted espresso) or a carajillo (coffee with a shot of liquor, often brandy or whisky). The bar counter at Bares is a great area to have your coffee while mingling with the locals.

3. Specialty coffee shops: Specialty coffee shops have become more prevalent in Spain in recent years, particularly in bigger cities like Barcelona and Madrid. These businesses emphasize the use of premium, ethically sourced beans and often employ talented baristas who create complex latte art. Coffee lovers looking for distinctive tastes and fragrances may choose from a variety of brewing techniques at specialty coffee shops, including pour-over and Aeropress.

4. Baking establishments (Panaderas) and pastry shops (Pasteleras): In

Spain, there are many bakeries and pastry shops that sell coffee in addition to delectable baked goodies. For a traditional Spanish breakfast, have a café con leche with your morning croissant.

5. hotel cafés: Hotel cafés are great locations for a leisurely cup of coffee since they often provide a calm atmosphere. These coffee shops provide a tranquil setting to sip your coffee while taking a break from touring, whether you're staying at the hotel or simply passing by.

6. Train Stations and Shopping Centers: Coffee chains like Starbucks and its regional counterparts are often found in larger shopping malls and railway stations. For tourists who are on the run, these locations provide quick coffee alternatives.

7. Outdoor cafés, or Terrazas: Outdoor cafés in Spain are called "Terrazas," and they are common in places like Barcelona and Seville. You may take in the sun and the bustling city while sipping your coffee on a terraza.

Every coffee aficionado may find their ideal cup in Spain, whether they want a classic café solo, a foamy café con leche, or a modern flat white. You won't be far from a beautiful café in Spain, whether you're in a big city or a quaint tiny hamlet.

CHAPTER 7

Top 15 local Cuisines to try in Spain

Spanish cuisine is renowned for its wide variety of regional dishes. Make sure to sample these top 15 regional foods and specialties while in Spain:

1. **Paella (Valencia):** A well-known rice dish prepared with saffron, vegetables, and an

assortment of proteins, such as chicken, rabbit, fish, or a combination of these. It is a Valencian institution.

2. Tapas (Andalusia): A variety of small, tasty foods, from olives and almonds to more elaborate fare like patatas bravas (fried potatoes in a hot tomato sauce) and jamón ibérico (cured ham).

3. Gazpacho: is a cool soup from Andalusia prepared with tomatoes, peppers, cucumbers, and onions. It is ideal for sweltering summer days.

4. Pulpo a la Gallega (Galicia): Octopus prepared with potatoes, paprika, and extra virgin olive oil. It is a specialty of Galicia.

5. Roasted suckling pig with crispy skin and delicate flesh, known as cochinillo asado (Segovia). This meal is well-known in Segovia.

6. Fabada Asturiana (Asturias): A filling bean stew prepared with white beans, chorizo, morcilla (blood sausage), and pork. It comes from northern Spain and is a hearty meal.

7. Tortilla Espanola: An omelette from Spain made with eggs, potatoes, and sometimes onions. It is a comfort dish and a standard tapa.

8. Crema Catalana (Catalonia): A dessert like crème brûlée but with cinnamon and lemon zest as the main flavors. This delicious treat hails from Catalonia.

9. Pisto (Castilla-La Mancha): This cuisine is a combination of sautéed vegetables such as tomatoes, peppers, zucchini, and onions and is similar to ratatouille.

10. Salmorejo (Andalusia): This cold tomato soup is thicker than gazpacho and often topped with jamón serrano and hard-boiled eggs.

11. Cocido Madrileño (Madrid): A filling stew made with chickpeas, vegetables, and different meat cuts, such as chorizo and morcilla.

12. Txuletón (Basque Country): a thick, grilled T-bone steak that is finished to perfection and seasoned just with coarse salt. Steaks are a specialty of the Basque Country.

13. Catalan calçots with Romesco sauce: Calçots are a seasonal delight that is grilled and then dipped in a creamy, nutty romesco sauce. They are comparable to green onions.

14. Bocadillo de Calamares (Madrid): A simple but delectable sandwich stuffed with golden-brown, deep-fried squid rings. In Madrid, it's a well-liked street snack.

15. Percebes (Galicia and Asturias): Also known as "goose barnacles," these odd-looking seafood treats are appreciated in northern Spain for their distinctive flavor.

Discovering these regional foods is like taking a gourmet tour of Spain's many regions and cultural heritage. Spanish food provides a fascinating culinary trip for your taste buds, whether you're enjoying paella by the seaside in Valencia or indulging in pintxos in San Sebastián.

CHAPTER 8

10-days Itinerary

Exploring the Best of Spain in a 10-Day Spanish Adventure

Spain's many regions, rich history, and lively culture may all be experienced in a 10-day tour. Here is a sample of what your wonderful trip to Spain may include.

Day 1: Entering Barcelona

Start your trip in Barcelona, the vivacious capital of Catalonia. You'll feel the vitality of the city as you land at El Prat Airport. Check into your hotel, leave your baggage there, take a moment to unwind, and then go out to explore. Examine the distinctive architecture of Antoni Gaud, including the recognizable Sagrada Famlia, as you stroll down the busy Las Ramblas, explore the ancient Gothic Quarter, and more.

Day 2: Explore Gaud's Masterworks

Spend the second day just looking at Antoni Gaud's creations. Explore the unique designs and expansive city vistas of Park Güell. Visit two more of Gaud's architectural marvels, Casa Milà and Casa Batlló. Dine on Catalan food at a nearby restaurant in the evening.

Day 3: a day trip to Montserrat

Visit Montserrat, a magnificent mountain range about one hour from Barcelona, on a day trip. Discover the Black Madonna's home at the Montserrat Monastery and stroll through stunning scenery. In the evening, return to Barcelona.

Day 4: Get to Valencia

Take a high-speed train to Valencia, a city renowned for its cutting-edge design and mouthwatering paella. Visit the historic Central Market, take in a paella meal, and explore the City of Arts and Sciences.

Day 5: Take a tour of Valencia

On your second day, take in more of Valencia's delights. Explore the magnificent Valencia Cathedral and climb the Miguelete Tower for sweeping views. Take it easy on Patacona and Malvarrosa's lovely beaches.

Day 6 Journey to Madrid

Take a train to the vibrant capital of Spain, Madrid. Visit the Royal Palace to start your Madrid exploration, then take a walk around the vivacious Puerta del Sol and Gran Va in the evening.

Day 7: Madrid's Art and Cultural Scene

Explore Madrid's art and culture on the seventh day. Observe the works of

Velázquez, Goya, and El Greco in the famed Prado Museum. At a bustling tapas bar in the evening, indulge in authentic Spanish food.

Day 8: includes a trip to Toledo.

Visit Toledo, a UNESCO World Heritage city with a long history, on a day excursion. The Toledo Cathedral, Alcázar, and Santa Maria la Blanca Synagogue are all worth seeing. For the evening, go back to Madrid.

Day 9: The Jewel of Andalusia, Seville

Fly to Seville, the capital of Andalusia, and savor the passionate mood there. Visit the magnificent Alcazar Palace, Seville Cathedral, and the old Barrio Santa Cruz neighborhood.

Day 10: Saying goodbye to Spain in Seville

On your last day in Spain, visit the charming Plaza de Espana, take a leisurely boat trip through Parque de Maria Luisa, and in the evening, take in a classic flamenco performance. At a nearby tapas bar, savor your last bite of Spanish food.

The departure day:

You'll take back memories of the vibrant architecture, delectable food, passionate culture, and friendly people as your 10-day trip around Spain concludes. Say goodbye to Spain, but know that its enchantment will live on forever in your heart.

A 10-day schedule in Spain offers a frenzy of experiences, from the cutting-edge streets of Barcelona to the historical treasures of Toledo and the ferocious passion of Seville. This trip across Spain's many landscapes and energetic towns is evidence of the nation's unique fabric of history, culture, and unspoiled natural beauty.

CHAPTER 9
Welcome To
Portugal

A Tapestry of Pure Beauty and Timeless Charm

Portugal, a gem of southern Europe, enchants visitors with its variety of scenery, rich history, and hospitable culture. Its ability to fluidly combine the past and present results in a tapestry that is both entrancing and beautiful.

Beachline splendor:

Portugal is known for its gorgeous coastline, which spans more than 800 kilometers along the Atlantic Ocean. Golden beaches are surrounded by craggy cliffs and turquoise seas in the southern region of the Algarve. With its recognizable sea arches and secret coves, Praia da Marinha is a prime example of the coastal beauty that attracts tourists from all over the globe.

Historically Significant:

The cities of Portugal are living museums with a rich past. The nation's capital, Lisbon, is a city of contrasts, with historic sites like the Belém Tower and Jerónimos Monastery serving as reminders of the nation's illustrious history as well as bustling areas like Alfama and Bairro Alto.

The ancient Port wine cellars and the well-preserved medieval old town of Porto, which lies tucked along the Douro River, are both world-famous attractions. In the middle of verdant woods and gardens, Sintra, a UNESCO World Heritage site, provides buildings that seem like they belong in a dream, such as the vibrant Pena Palace and the enigmatic Quinta da Regaleira.

Cultural Abundance:

The music of Portugal, known as Fado, captures the essence of the country and is a source of pride for the country. The somber melodies and heart-wrenching lyrics explore themes of yearning and saudade, a profound emotional condition that is distinctive to Portuguese culture. For a full understanding of this cultural gem, you must see a Fado performance in a Lisbon pub.

Culinary delights include:

Portuguese food is a celebration of tastes and ingredients that come from both the land and the sea. Portuguese cuisine is a delectable voyage that ranges from the traditional pastéis de nata, rich custard pastries, to robust meals like bacalhau à brás (salted fish). World-class wines are produced in the country's wine regions, such as the Douro Valley and Alentejo, and they go well with the food.

Natural marvels include:

Portugal has a variety of sceneries inland as well as

along the coast. Terraced wineries in the Douro Valley give breathtaking views, while the Azores and Madeira archipelagos provide volcanic scenery, lush woods, and unusual species. In the Algarve, the Ria Formosa Natural Park is a paradise for birdwatchers, while in the north, the Peneda-Gerês National Park provides trekking through pure nature.

Pleasant Hospitality:

Portugal's people are what make it beautiful. Portuguese people are known for their warm welcomes to guests and their famous hospitality. Travelers are made to feel at home by the Portuguese people's sincere warmth and openness.

The beauty of Portugal goes beyond its natural surroundings to include its population, culture, history, and culinary customs. Time appears to pass more slowly in this nation, luring visitors to cherish each minute and unearth the hidden wonders

that make Portugal a
veritable treasure trove of
adventures. Portugal's beauty
is a constant companion,
making an ever-lasting
impression on those who
have the luxury to come,
whether they are seeing
ancient cities, relaxing on
stunning beaches, or
indulging in mouthwatering
food.

CHAPTER 10

The interesting facts about
Portugal
Portugal is a fascinating
European nation with a
lively culture and a rich
history. It is a popular travel
destination because of its
distinctive features. Here are
some intriguing facts about
Portugal:

Exploration

Period: Portugal sometimes
refers to the period between
the 15th and 16th centuries
as the "Age of Exploration"
since it was a crucial part of
worldwide discovery.
Portugal became a major

player during the Age of Discovery thanks to Portuguese explorers like Vasco da Gama and Ferdinand Magellan, who helped build Portuguese territories and discover new marine routes.

The Oldest Borders in the World Portugal is one of the world's oldest countries with continuous boundaries since its borders haven't altered much since 1139. The nation has been able to maintain its own culture and customs because of this stability.

Port Wine Only made in the Douro Valley, Port wine is famously manufactured in Portugal. This fortified, sweet wine is matured in Porto city cellars and has long been regarded as a representation of Portuguese enology.

The capital of Cork With cork oak woods making up around one-third of the world's total cork forest area, Portugal is the world's greatest producer of cork. Wine stoppers, fashion items, and even spaceship heat shielding are among the goods that employ cork.

The earliest university is One of Europe's oldest institutions, the University of Coimbra was established in 1290 and is now a UNESCO World Heritage site. The Joanina Library, a historic library, is home to precious volumes and manuscripts.

Fado music Fado, a profoundly emotive subgenre of Portuguese music, is sometimes referred to as the country's soul. This emotive and depressing music is played in both intimate bars and large concert halls, and it is recognized by UNESCO as an Intangible Cultural Heritage.

Lisbon's Heritage Trams Lisbon is famed for its distinctive yellow trams, such as the well-known Tram 28, which travels through the city's ancient districts and provides a distinctive and endearing way to explore Lisbon's streets.

Madeira's Magnificent Landscape The Portuguese island of Madeira, an autonomous province, is renowned for its breathtaking natural beauty, which includes towering cliffs, verdant woods, and terraced vineyards. Excellent hiking paths may be found along the Levada irrigation systems.

Language Legacy Portugal, Brazil, Mozambique, Angola, Cape Verde, Guinea-Bissau, East Timor, and Equatorial Guinea all have Portuguese as their official language. It is among the languages that are most often spoken throughout the globe.

Cabo da Roca Europe's westernmost point, Cabo da Roca, is located in Portugal. Because guests can stand on the cliffs and stare out at the Atlantic Ocean, this place is well-known for its stunning sunsets.

Football Glory Football has a long history in Portugal, which has produced stars like Cristiano Ronaldo. The national team, referred to as the Seleço, won both the UEFA Nations League and the UEFA European Championship in 2016.

Gastronomic Delights Portuguese food is excellent and diversified. Famous foods include feijoada (a robust bean stew), pastéis de nata (custard tarts), and bacalhau à brás (salted fish). Additionally, seafood dishes like seafood rice and grilled sardines are popular in Portugal.

These amazing facts about Portugal demonstrate the country's historical importance, natural beauty, cultural diversity, and contributions to the world, making it a compelling and welcoming destination for tourists from across the globe. Portugal's harmonious fusion of history and contemporary never ceases to wow tourists with its enduring allure.

Geography Of Portugal

Coastal beauty and a variety of landscapes characterize Portugal's geography.

Portugal, located in the southwest of the Iberian Peninsula, has a varied topography that includes coastal plains, rocky mountains, and lush valleys. Portugal's geography's main characteristics are as follows:

Start with the coast. Over 800 kilometers of the country's breathtaking Atlantic Ocean coastline run along its length. Dramatic cliffs, pristine beaches, and charming coves define the shoreline. For its immaculate beaches and limestone formations, the Algarve area in the south of the nation is especially well-known.

Mountains and mountain ranges: Mountain ranges may be found all around the nation. With a height of 2,351 meters (7,713 feet) above sea level, Mount Pico on the island of Pico in the Azores archipelago is the tallest mountain. The tallest mountain range in a continental country is the Serra da Estrela in Portugal.

River Valleys: In Portugal, there are several rich river valleys, notably the Douro Valley, which is well-known for its terraced vineyards that produce Port wine. Lisbon and the heart of Portugal are traversed by the Tagus River, the longest river on the Iberian Peninsula.

The plateaus: Vast grasslands and plateaus are a feature of the Alentejo area of southern Portugal. The agricultural activities and rustic scenery of this area are well-known.

Islands: The Azores and Madeira are the two most notable of the many archipelagos that Portugal contains in **the Atlantic Ocean**. In addition to their diverse wildlife, these islands include lush foliage and volcanic sceneries.

Forests and Parks: Forests like cork oak, pine, and eucalyptus groves often cover Portugal's terrain. Along with displaying the nation's biodiversity and natural beauty, there are a lot of parks and protected places in nature.

Climate Of Portugal

Portugal's climate varies depending on the region and is influenced by the Mediterranean.

Most of Portugal is subject to a Mediterranean climate, which is typified by hot, dry summers and warm, rainy winters. As a result of the country's varied terrain, there is noticeable regional climatic variance. Following are Portugal's climatic zones:

Mediterranean Climate: Lisbon and the Algarve are among the coastal areas that benefit from the Mediterranean climate. Winters are moderate and moist, but summers are hot and dry with frequent highs of 30°C (86°F).

Interior Plains: Inland areas, like the Alentejo, have a more continental climate with hotter summers and colder winters. Winters may be frigid, but summertime highs can go far beyond 35°C (95°F).

Mountainous Areas: Portugal's mountainous regions, like the Serra da Estrela, have cooler temperatures, particularly in the winter, and get a lot of snowfall.

Azores and Madeira, respectively: In contrast to Madeira, which has a subtropical climate with moderate winters and warm summers, the Azores have mild temperatures all year round.

Rainfall: Because of the Atlantic Ocean's impact on Portugal's climate, the country experiences heavy rainfall, particularly in its northern and western parts.

It is often dryer towards the south and east of the nation.

Portugal is a fantastic location for a variety of outdoor activities, including hiking in the mountains of the Azores, wine tasting in the Douro Valley, and beach holidays in the Algarve thanks to its diverse topography and temperature. Every tourist may find enjoyment in its varied landscapes and climatic conditions.

Culture Of Portugal

Portugal, a country in Europe that sits on the westernmost point of the Iberian Peninsula, has a rich and varied cultural legacy that has been influenced by many different civilizations throughout history and discovery. Portuguese friendliness, a feeling of national pride, and a great respect for artistic, musical, and gastronomic traditions are what define Portuguese culture.

Music and dance.

In Portugal, fado music is perhaps the most well-known and intensely emotive style. It often is played in private situations and generally has depressing lyrics. Particularly in Lisbon, the famed Fado homes are popular gathering places for residents and visitors to listen to this soul-stirring music.

Portugal also has a long history of folk music, which is influenced by the distinct musical traditions of the many regions. The country's rural background is reflected in the folk dance ensembles, or ranchos folclóricos, which perform traditional dances and wear vibrant costumes.

Celebrations & Festivals:

The nation of Portugal has various festivals all year long because Portuguese people love to party. The most well-known ones are as follows:

Carnival: Carnaval is an occasion for revelry and fancy dress, and it is celebrated with vivid street celebrations and colorful parades. Famous for their lavish Carnaval festivities are the towns of Ovar and Loulé.

San Joao Festival This event honors St. John the Baptist and is held on June 23rd in Porto. It is a huge street celebration with fireworks, music, and the customary head-bashing of revelers with plastic hammers.

Fado Festivals In Portugal, there are several Fado events where well-known musicians and up-and-coming performers alike provide riveting performances.

Cuisine

The country's marine heritage and varied landscapes are reflected in Portuguese cuisine. A lot of the cuisine is made with seafood; typical meals include grilled sardines and salted codfish, or bacalhau. The pastel de nata (custard tart), a beloved treat, is one of Portugal's other well-known pastries.

The Douro Valley's world-famous Port wine is only one of the many wines produced in Portugal, which has a long history of embracing the beverage. Wine is also an important component of Portuguese culture. There are many great chances for wine tourism in wine areas like the Douro, Alentejo, and Vinho Verde.

Visual arts and architecture

Roman, Moorish, Gothic, and Manueline architectural styles have all affected Portugal's rich architectural history. UNESCO World Heritage Sites that display the exquisite Manueline architecture are the Tower of Belém and the Jerónimos Monastery in Lisbon.

The art world has benefited greatly from the work of Portuguese artists as well. Famous examples of Portuguese art include José Malhoa's paintings and

Amadeo de Souza-Cardoso's modernist creations.

Literature

Fernando Pessoa, a famous novelist from Portugal noted for his original and philosophical writing, is the country's most well-known author. Portuguese as a language has a strong cultural effect because of its lovely poetry and lyrical features.

In conclusion, the history, music, gastronomy, and art of Portugal are woven together to create a unique culture. Visitors to Portugal are made to feel at home by the country's kind and open residents, and the year-round excitement is guaranteed by the thriving cultural life of the nation. Visitors and residents alike continue to be enthralled and inspired by Portugal's rich cultural history.

CHAPTER 11

Visa Requirements To Visit Portugal

Depending on your nationality, Portugal in 2024 will have different visa requirements. You should be aware that different nationalities have different rules while visiting Portugal for up to 90 days in 180 days. The essential details are broken out as follows:

Visa-Free Entry: Portugal does not need a visa for tourists or brief visits of up to 90 days within 180 days for nationals of the majority of European countries, including those in the European Union and Schengen Area. Travelers from the United States, Canada, Australia, New Zealand, and Japan are also covered by this insurance.

Application for a Visa: If you are not from one of those nations where visa requirements are free, you must submit an application for a visa at the Portuguese embassy or consulate in their place of origin or in the nation where they are legally residing.

The necessity to contact the Portuguese embassy or consulate for specific visa application requirements must be emphasized. These requirements may change based on your country of origin and the reason for your stay.

Standard   Visa Requirements: Typically, the following papers are needed to get a visa to Portugal:

- an active passport.
- submitting   a completed   visa application.
- two current passport-size pictures must be sent.
- confirmation of travel protection.
- confirmation   of lodging arrangements, such as an Airbnb

reservation or a hotel reservation.

- proof that you have enough money to meet your costs throughout your stay in Portugal.
- Additional Documentation: Additional paperwork may be required, depending on the reason for your visit. These can include a formal letter of invitation or one outlining the reason for your visit.

Basic Things To Know Before Visiting Portugal

To guarantee a successful and pleasurable journey, it is necessary to get acquainted with certain fundamental facts before traveling to Portugal. What you should know is as follows:

1. Location and geography

Portugal is a country on the Iberian Peninsula in

southwest Europe. Its eastern boundary is with Spain, while its western and southern boundaries are with the Atlantic Ocean. Portuguese is the country's official language, and Lisbon is its main city.

2. Currency: Portugal uses the Euro (€) as its unit of exchange. Despite the widespread acceptance of credit and debit cards, it's still a good idea to have some cash on hand for smaller transactions and in case you visit locations where cards may not be accepted.

3. Time Zone Western European Time (WET), which is UTC+0 in the winter and UTC+1 in the summer when daylight saving time is in effect, is the time zone used in Portugal.

4. Climate and weather Portugal has moderate, rainy winters and hot, dry summers due to its Mediterranean climate. While the interior regions may sometimes suffer more severe temperature changes, the coastal areas typically have more mild temperatures. For your precise trip dates and destinations, be sure to check the weather forecast.

5. Visa and entry prerequisites You could need a visa to enter Portugal depending on your nationality (see previous answer for information). Make sure your passport is valid for at least six months after the day you want to travel.

6. Health and Safety: Portugal is often regarded as a secure location for tourists. But just as in any other nation, it's important to be on the lookout for and take precautions against small-time theft and pickpocketing, particularly in busy tourist locations. High-quality healthcare is provided, and no special vaccines are needed to enter.

7. Transportation Portugal has a sophisticated transportation system. Cities may be reached by automobile, bus, or rail. In metropolitan regions, there is a wide variety of public transit options, including trams and buses. Portugal has several airports, with the main international entry points being Lisbon Airport (LIS) and Porto Airport (OPO).

8 Language: Although English is frequently spoken in tourist regions and many people employed in the tourism sector are fluent in it, Portuguese is the official language.

9. Culinary: Portuguese food is excellent and diversified. Make sure to sample regional specialties like grilled sardines, pastéis de nata, and bacalhau (salted codfish). Port wine and Vinho Verde are two of Portugal's well-known wines.

10. Cultural Standards: Portugal's

population is renowned for their kind hospitality. A handshake with the phrases "please" and "thank you" (por favor and obrigado/obrigada) are typical greetings. Tipping is often approximately 10% of the tab in restaurants.

11.   Electrical power: Portugal makes use of electrical outlets with the Europlug Type C and Type F plugs with 230V and 50Hz as the default voltage and frequency. You may need a plug adapter and/or voltage converter if your gadgets require a different voltage or plug type.

12.   Emergency Numbers: The police, ambulance, and fire services emergency number in Portugal is 112.

Keep in mind that Portugal is a diversified nation with a thriving cultural history, breathtaking scenery, and a warm attitude. Traveling there and taking in its stunning scenery, historic cities, and lively culture may be a fascinating and educational experience.

Best Time To Visit Spain for the best experience

Depending on your interests and the areas you want to visit, there may be an ideal time to go to Spain. Because of Spain's varied terrain and climate, each season offers its own unique experiences. For each season, take into account the following:

1. Spring, from March To May:

Traveling to Spain in the spring is fantastic. Generally speaking, the weather is warm, and many places have comfortable temperatures. Exploring cities like Barcelona, Madrid, Seville, and Valencia, trekking in the Pyrenees, and visiting Andalusian towns like Granada and Cordoba are all very enjoyable during this season. The country's landscapes come alive with vibrant blooms in the spring.

2. During the summer (June to August):

The summer months are the busiest travel times in Spain, particularly in the Balearic Islands (Ibiza, Mallorca, etc.) and other coastal regions like the Costa del Sol and Costa Brava. Vacations at the beach are a fantastic fit for the hot, dry weather. However, temperatures in places like Madrid and Seville may get beyond 90°F (32°C) often. Summer is the ideal season to visit if you appreciate exciting nightlife and busy beach scenes.

3. Autumn, September To November:

Spain is beautiful in the fall, particularly in September and October. The weather is still beautiful as the summer throngs begin to dissipate. This is a fantastic time for wine lovers to tour La Rioja's vineyards or take part in traditional activities like the grape harvest festivities (vendimias). The Pyrenees and northern areas also have beautiful autumn foliage.

4. Winter, December To February:

If you wish to go to Spain in a season of warmer temperatures and less tourist traffic, the winter is a great time to do it. Winter sun getaways are suitable in coastal areas with mild winters, such as the Canary Islands and the Costa del Sol. While northern and mountainous locales may be fairly chilly and provide skiing possibilities, Mediterranean towns like Barcelona and Valencia can enjoy comparatively moderate winters.

5. Festivals and Events period: When making travel plans, take into account the festivals and events you want to attend. Spain is renowned for its colorful celebrations, like the Running of the Bulls in Pamplona, Semana Santa processions in Seville and other towns, and La Tomatina (the tomato tossing festival) in Buol. If you wish to attend or observe these activities, be sure to schedule your trip to coincide with the appropriate dates.

The ideal time to go to Spain ultimately depends on your choices and the experiences you want to have. With excellent weather and fewer visitors, spring and fall are often regarded as the most comfortable and delightful periods for a well-rounded stay. However, if you like going to the beach, summer may be your favorite season, while winter is great for getting away from colder locations and enjoying milder temps in certain areas.

Basic Portuguese phrases to interact with the locals

A few simple Portuguese words can make it easier for you to communicate with locals and improve your trip to Portugal. Portuguese is widely spoken in Portugal, particularly in tourist regions, but even a small amount of Portuguese is appreciated and may go a long way. To get you started, review these fundamental Portuguese words and phrases:

Greetings:
- Hello: Olá (oh-LAH)
- Good morning: Bom dia (bohm DEE-ah)
- Good afternoon: Boa tarde (boh-ah TAHR-day)
- Good evening/night: Boa noite (boh-ah NOH-ee-tay)
- Goodbye: Adeus (ah-DAY-oos) or Tchau (chow)

Polite Expressions:
- Please: Por favor (pohr fah-VOHR)
- Thank you: Obrigado (oh-bree-GAH-doo) if you're male, or Obrigada (oh-bree-GAH-dah) if you're female
- Yes: Sim (seem)
- No: Não (now)

Basic Questions:

- How are you?: Cómo está? (KOH-moo es-TAH?)
- What's your name?: Qual é o seu nome? (kwahl eh oo seh-oo NOH-may?)
- Where is...?: Onde fica...? (OHN-day FEE-kah...?)
- How much is this?: Quanto custa isto? (KWAN-toh KOOS-tah EES-too?)

Getting Around:

- Excuse me: Com licença (kohm lee-SAYN-sah)
- I'm lost: Estou perdido (ess-TOH pehr-DEE-doo)
- Can you help me?: Pode ajudar-me? (POH-day ah-joo-DAR-may?)
- Where is the restroom?: Onde fica a casa de banho? (OHN-day FEE-kah ah KA-sah deh BAH-nyoh?)

Food and Dining:

- Menu: Menu (MEH-noo)
- Water: Água (AH-gwah)
- Coffee: Café (kah-FAY)
- I would like...: Gostaria de... (gohs-TAH-ree-ah day...)
- The bill, please: A conta, por favor
- (ah KOHN-tah, pohr fah-VOHR)

6. Shopping:

- How much does this cost?: Quanto custa isto? (KWAN-toh KOOS-tah EES-too?)
- I would like to buy this: Gostaria de comprar isto (gohs-TAH-ree-ah day kohm-PRAR EES-too)
- Do you accept credit cards?: Aceitam cartões de crédito? (ah-say-TAHM kar-TOHNS day KRAY-dee-toh?)

7. Numbers:

1: Um (oom)
2: Dois (doh-ees)

169

3: Três (traysh)
10: Dez (daysh)
100: Cem (saym)

It's important to keep in mind that Portuguese pronunciation might be a little challenging, but it's always appreciated when people try to speak in their tongue. When someone is learning Portuguese, native speakers are often very patient and kind. Have a great time while you're there!

<u>CHAPTER 12</u>

Getting Around Portugal for the first time of visit

Getting about this stunning nation is rather simple owing to its well-developed transportation system. Here is a travel guide to Portugal to help you have an enjoyable and trouble-free trip:

1. Travel via Air:

Arrival: The majority of travelers from outside the country land at the airports in Lisbon (Aeroporto Humberto Delgado) or Porto (Francisco Sá Carneiro Airport). Major cities in Portugal and Europe may be reached easily by plane from either airport.

Domestic Flights: To save time if your plan covers many destinations, you may want to think about using domestic flights. Popular domestic carriers include Ryanair and TAP Air Portugal.

2. Trains

Intercity Trains: CP (Comboios de Portugal) runs Portugal's huge and effective rail network. Lisbon, Porto, and Faro are just a few of the important cities connected by the Intercidades and Alfa Pendular trains. These trains are cozy and have beautiful scenery.

Urban Trains: The CP Urbanos de Lisboa trains in Lisbon are a practical method to see the suburbs.

The Metro do Porto allows you to get through the city of Porto.

Train tickets may be purchased at stations, online, or via the CP smartphone app. It is essential to make reservations in advance, particularly during busy tourist seasons.

3. Buses:

Buses for Long-Distance Travel: The two major bus operators for long-distance travel between cities are Rede Expressos and Citi Express. Buses are often pleasant and well-maintained, and they provide an affordable way to see the nation.

Local Buses: Within cities, public buses are a great method to go to places where the metro or rail system does not go.

4. Trams and the Metro:

Lisbon: The capital's metro system makes it easy to go about. Trams are recognizable and provide a distinctive experience, particularly the ancient Tram 28.

Porto: The city's metro system is effective for getting about, and trams are also an option.

5. Hiring a Vehicle:

Exploring Remote Areas: Renting a vehicle might be a terrific alternative if you want to go to remote or difficult-to-reach areas like the Algarve or the Douro Valley. At airports and in city centers, reputable automobile rental agencies are present.

Parking: In old city centers, parking may be a problem. Find park-and-ride

facilities or open parking lots.

6. Ride-Sharing and Taxis:

In large cities and popular tourist destinations, taxis are widely accessible. Make sure the meter is on at all times.

In Portugal, ride-sharing services like Uber are available, offering a practical and often less expensive alternative to taxis.

7. Boats and Ferries:

The coastline and rivers of Portugal provide options for ferry rides and boat adventures. Consider taking a ferry from Lisbon to Almada or Trafaria to cross the Tagus River.

You can view Porto from a different angle by taking a boat cruise down the Douro River.

8. Cycling and walking

The greatest way to see cities and towns in Portugal is often on foot. You may immerse yourself in the local culture and find hidden treasures by walking.

There are designated bicycle lanes in several cities, like Lisbon and Porto, and bike rentals are offered for a leisurely ride along the shoreline.

9. Language-Related Issues:

Even though English is widely spoken in Portugal, particularly in tourist regions, learning a few simple Portuguese phrases may be useful and well-liked by locals.

Travel cards

10. Take into account buying transportation permits or cards that provide unrestricted travel during certain times. If you often use public transit, these may help you save money.

Portugal's transportation network is effective and varied, making it convenient for first-time travelers and pleasurable. You may utilize trains, buses, metros, taxis, or even a rental vehicle to easily tour this fascinating nation, depending on your plan and interests.

Practical Steps To Stay Safe and healthy in Portugal

To guarantee an enjoyable and stress-free journey, it is important to be safe and healthy when visiting Portugal. Here are some useful actions to keep you safe and comfortable while you're there:

1. Purchase comprehensive travel insurance that

includes coverage for medical emergencies, trip cancellations, and lost or stolen property. A copy of your insurance policy and a list of emergency contacts should be kept on hand.

2. vaccines and Health Precautions: Check to see that you have had all of your recommended vaccines. If there are any suggested vaccines or health measures related to your travel to Portugal, see your healthcare professional.

Although Portugal is often free of tropical illnesses, it is always advisable to take precautions against mosquito bites, particularly if you want to go to remote locations or during mosquito season.

3. Remind Hydrated: If you're traveling to Portugal during the summer, it's particularly vital to remain hydrated since the country may experience hot, sunny weather. Always have a refillable water bottle with you.

4. Sun Protection: Due to Portugal's potential for extreme sun exposure, you should use sunglasses, a wide-brimmed hat, and sunscreen with a high SPF rating to prevent sunburn and UV rays damage.

5. Food and Water Safety: Portugal is well recognized for its delectable cuisine, but use caution while eating on the street or at local markets. Ensure that food is cooked thoroughly and served at a safe temperature. Drink bottled or tap water that you are certain is safe to consume. Tap water is generally safe in metropolitan places, but it's advisable to double-check with neighbors or your lodging.

6. Prescription drugs and first aid: Bring a copy of your prescription and any prescription drugs you may need. A basic first-aid kit including necessities like bandages, painkillers, and any over-the-counter drugs you often use is also a good idea to have on hand.

7. Have a list of emergency contacts: including your country's embassy or consulate, local emergency numbers (dial 112 for police, medical help, and fire services), and the contact information for your travel insurance company.

8. Use hotel safes or strong locks to protect your valuables and critical papers (such as your passport, travel insurance, etc.). To avoid pickpocketing, use caution in busy situations.

9. Stay Informed: Maintain awareness of local safety and health warnings as well as current happenings. Observe the guidance provided by your embassy or consulate and the local authorities.

10. Local Laws and traditions: To guarantee polite conduct, familiarize yourself with local laws and traditions. For instance, it's normal to shake hands when greeting someone and, as was previously noted, to use polite language.

By following these sensible recommendations, you may travel to Portugal in safety and health while soaking in its rich culture, stunning scenery, and welcoming people. To guarantee a fun and trouble-free trip, always be alert to your surroundings and use common sense when you're out and about.

Do's And Don'ts In Portugal

To guarantee a courteous and pleasurable trip, it's crucial to be knowledgeable about the regional traditions, manners, and cultural standards before traveling to Portugal. Following are some guidelines to follow:

In Portugal, you should:

1. Welcome with courtesy. Polite greetings are appreciated by the Portuguese. Salutations such as "Bom dia" (good morning), "Boa tarde" (good afternoon), and "Boa noite" (good evening/night) should be used as appropriate.

2. Use courteous language Requests should be made with "Por favor" (please) and "Obrigado" (thank you), or "Obrigada" if you are a woman. Being courteous is highly regarded.

3. Respect regional customs: It's common to offer a modest gift, such as wine, chocolates, or flowers, as a sign of thanks while visiting someone's house.

4. Be Properly Attired: Dress modestly and cover your knees and shoulders while visiting places of worship. In fancy restaurants and events, it's also a good idea to dress respectfully.

5. Savor Local Cuisine: Try some traditional Portuguese cuisine and beverages. Custard tarts, salted codfish, and fresh seafood from the area are not to be missed.

5. Tipping: In restaurants, cafés, and cabs, tipping is customary. It's nice to leave a tip of around 10%. However, check the bill first since some establishments impose service fees.

7.   Utilize   public transportation: The public transportation system in Portugal is effective. Explore cities like Lisbon and Porto by using the trams, buses, and subway.

Practice good manners by waiting until other people have finished speaking in a discussion before answering. Being kind and patient are desirable qualities.

In Portugal Don'ts:

1 Don't rush Portuguese, folks often keep more flexible hours. Avoid hurrying service personnel, and don't be in a hurry.

2.   Don't   Wear Inappropriate Clothing: In public places such as churches and restaurants, avoid wearing swimsuits or other provocative attire.

3.   Don't   Talk   Too Loud: Loud displays of conduct in public are often discouraged. When speaking in public, keep your voice at a manageable level.

4. Refrain from touching artifacts: Avoid touching antiques or displays unless specifically permitted while visiting churches, historical sites, or museums.

5. Don't Interrupt Meals: Show respect for mealtimes and refrain from speaking to natives while they are eating. The largest and often most leisurely meal of the day is lunch.

6. Don't Ignore Local Wines: Avoid ordering just foreign selections while eating out since Portugal is known for its wines. Ask for suggestions and sample some local wines.

7. Remember to pay for bread and snacks: For the bread and appetizers that are given to the table, certain restaurants may charge a little surcharge. Check your bill since it's customary to do so.

8. Avoid Casual Discussion of Politics and Religion: Politics and religion are delicate subjects that should not be discussed unless you are among a small group of people you can trust.

9. Don't Litter: Portugal has made an effort to maintain the cleanliness of its urban centers and outdoor spaces. Be environmentally conscious and place rubbish in appropriate containers.

To maintain good relationships with the locals, keep in mind that being kind, patient, and respectful of local customs will go a long way.

CHAPTER 12

Interesting Things To Do In Portugal

travelers may enjoy a wide range of intriguing and entertaining activities in portugal. Everyone can find something to enjoy, regardless of their interests in history, culture, nature, or adventure. some of the most intriguing activities in portugal are listed below:

1. explore lisbon: the capital of Portugal, lisbon, is a dynamic, historic city with a lot to see and do. visit the ancient belém tower and jerónimos monastery, stroll through the alfama neighborhood's winding lanes, and take a tram ride across the city's recognizable hills.

2. explore porto: porto, the second-largest city in portugal, is well-known for the ribeira, a scenic riverbank neighborhood. visit the livraria lello, a gorgeous bookshop, and enjoy a tour of the port wine cellars in vila nova de gaia. Also, explore the old city center.

3. go to sintra: sintra, a unesco world heritage site, is renowned for its beautiful 19th-century architecture, notably the eye-catching pena palace and the moorish castle. The village is a fantastic day excursion from Lisbon since it is surrounded by thick woods.

4. take in the algarve beaches: beautiful beaches may be found in the algarve area of southern portugal. explore quaint seaside villages like lagos and albufeira while unwinding on the golden dunes and swimming in the pristine waters.

5. sample Portuguese cuisine: enjoy classic Portuguese fare including grilled sardines, custard tarts, and salted codfish (bacalhau). don't forget to provide local wines like port wine and vinho verde with your meals.

6. wine tasting in the douro valley: the douro valley, one of the oldest wine-producing areas in the world, is well-known for its terraced vines. take a wine tour to experience the famed port wine of the area as well as other good wines while taking in the gorgeous countryside.

7. take a trip to the azores: In the center of the Atlantic Ocean, on an archipelago called the azores, breathtaking natural beauty may be found. in this far-off and undeveloped location, go to volcanic craters, cool yourself in thermal springs, and go whale watching.

8. travel to évora and the alentejo: évora, a unesco-designated city in the alentejo, is renowned for its intact roman temple and medieval city center. discover this lovely town's past and present.

9. surfing at nazaré: nazaré is well known for its enormous waves, making it a popular destination for large-wave surfers. It's fascinating to see the waves from the cliffs, even if you don't surf.

10. trek in the peneda-gerês national park: this national park, which can be found in northern portugal, has wonderful hiking options. while viewing animals and taking part in outdoor activities, explore lush woods, beautiful rivers, and spectacular scenery.

11. fado music in coimbra: fado music, which is known for its melancholy and lyrical songs, is well-known in coimbra. visit one of the city's historic fado houses to see a performance.

12. discover the island of madeira: the lush, hilly island of madeira is renowned for its beautiful scenery, hiking paths, and botanical gardens. take advantage of the levada walks, which lead you through beautiful irrigation canals.

Portugal has a lot to offer, from historical cities and stunning beaches to recreational pursuits and cultural explorations. Every tourist may find something intriguing in Portugal, whether they are interested in history, cuisine, or the natural world.

Beaches To Explore in Portugal

Every kind of tourist may find a nice beach in Portugal

thanks to its diversified shoreline. Here are a few of Portugal's most beautiful and interesting beaches to visit:

1. Praia da Rocha in the Algarve: Praia da Rocha, which lies in the Algarve, is one of Portugal's most well-known and popular beaches. It is known for its golden beaches, stunning cliffs, and pure seas. A bustling promenade with eateries, bars, and stores surrounds the beach.

2. Praia do Marinha in the Algarve: Praia do Marinha is often cited as one of Europe's most stunning beaches. There are gorgeous limestone cliffs, undiscovered caverns, and crystal-clear turquoise seas there. Swimming and snorkeling are excellent on the beach.

3. Praia do Ursa, Sintra: Praia da Ursa is a popular tourist destination because of its untamed beauty. The reward is a gorgeous, isolated beach surrounded by stunning cliffs and rock formations, yet getting there requires a difficult trek.

4. Praia do Guincho, Cascais: Praia do Guincho is a popular spot for windsurfers and kitesurfers because of its high winds, which are located just outside of Lisbon. The expansive area of golden sand is bordered by pine trees and dunes.

5. Praia da Dona Ana, Lagos: This picture-perfect beach is located close to Lagos in the Algarve. There are magnificent rock formations, beautiful lakes, and golden beaches there. Excellent swimming and snorkeling opportunities are there.

6. Praia da Comporta in Alentejo: is Alentejo's Praia da Comporta is renowned for its clean, unpolluted beauty. Dunes and rice farms surround the long, sandy beach. It's the perfect location for anyone looking for peace.

7. Praia do Camilo, Lagos: This hidden treasure is close to Lagos and is distinguished by its wooden steps that descend to the beach. The beach is ideal for snorkeling and is flanked by beautiful rocks.

8. Praia de Miramar, Porto: Praia de Miramar is well-known for the stunning Capela do Senhor da Pedra, a little church constructed on a rock formation at the edge of the beach. It's a distinctive and lovely location.

9. Praia do Falesia, Algarve: Praia da Falesia is renowned for its breathtaking red cliffs that contrast well with the golden dunes and turquoise water. It is located close to Albufeira. There is plenty of room to unwind and take in the sights on the long beach.

10. Praia da Nazaré, Nazaré: Praia da Nazaré draws large wave surfers from all over the globe because of its tremendous waves. Additionally, it has a picturesque coastal promenade and a beautiful fishing hamlet.

11. Praia de Carcavelos is One of the most well-liked beaches close to Lisbon which is located in Cascais. It is a favored location for both residents and visitors since it provides a significant stretch of sandy coastline.

The coastline of Portugal is diverse and beautiful, providing a variety of beach experiences from quiet and isolated to noisy and exciting. Every beach fan may find something to enjoy on Portugal's beaches, whether they are looking for leisure, water activities, or beautiful views.

Historical Sites In Portugal

Portugal has a long and illustrious past, and many historical sites in the country showcase its rich cultural legacy and the vital part it played in global exploration and commerce. Here is a list of some of Portugal's most significant historical locations:

1. Monastery of Jerónimos (Mosteiro dos Jerónimos), Lisbon: The Jerónimos Monastery, which was built in the 16th century, is a masterpiece of Manueline architecture and a UNESCO World Heritage Site. Its elaborate stone carvings include nautical themes and Christian iconography, and it was constructed to commemorate Portugal's Age of Discovery.

2. Belém Tower in Lisbon (Torre de Belém): The Belém Tower, which was constructed in the early 16th century, is yet another well-known illustration of Manueline design. It played a crucial role during the Age of Exploration as a stronghold to protect the entrance to Lisbon's port.

3. Tower of Tomar (Convent of Christ), Tomar: The Convent of Christ in Tomar was established by the Templar Knights in the 12th century and subsequently remodeled by the Order of Christ. It is also a UNESCO World Heritage Site. It is renowned for combining Templar and Renaissance architectural styles unusually.

4. University of Coimbra in Coimbra, Portugal: One of the oldest institutions in Europe is the University of Coimbra, which was established in 1290. A UNESCO World Heritage Site, its historic complex includes a stately Royal Palace and a library of Baroque architecture.

5. Castle of the Moors in Sintra (Castelo dos Mouros): This Sintra castle from the eighth century gives spectacular all-encompassing views of the region. It was constructed while the Moors were in charge and has a lengthy Reconquista history.

6. The Templo Romano in Évora, Portugal, One of the most notable Roman buildings in Portugal and a reminder of the nation's historical past is this well-preserved Roman temple from the first century AD.

7. Pena Palace (Palácio da Pena), located in Sintra: Sintra's Pena Palace is a Romanticist castle perched on a hill. It is vibrant and quirky. The 19th-century construction is currently recognized as a UNESCO World Heritage Site.

8. The Castle of the Knights Templar in Tomar, also known as Castelo dos Templários, was constructed in the 12th century by the Templar Knights and afterwards enlarged by the Order of Christ. It represents the presence of the Templars in Portugal.

9. The Roman ruins in Conimbriga, Condeixa-a-Nova, are as follows: One of Portugal's best-preserved Roman archaeological sites is Conimbriga. Visitors may visit mosaics, baths, and other historic buildings that have been kept beautifully.

10. Alcobaça Monastery, also known as Mosteiro de Alcobaça: The Alcobaça Monastery, a UNESCO World Heritage Site with beautiful Gothic architecture, was established in the 12th century. The graves of Pedro I and Inês de Castro, a sad couple in Portuguese history, are located there.

These historical locations provide a window into Portugal's extensive and varied past, which spans from its early Roman legacy through the Age of Exploration and the Renaissance's creative apogee. Each location offers a distinct tale and adds to the cultural history and character of the nation.

Top Museums and galleries in Portugal

Numerous museums and galleries in Portugal display the country's extensive cultural, historical, and artistic legacy. The best museums and art galleries in the nation are listed below for your perusal:

1. The Museu Nacional de Arte Antiga in Lisbon, Portugal, is the nation's first museum of ancient art. A sizable collection of Portuguese and European artwork from the Middle Ages to the 19th century is on display in this museum. Highlights include pieces by European masters and Portuguese artists.

2. The Calouste Gulbenkian Museum in Lisbon (Museu Calouste Gulbenkian): The Gulbenkian Museum is home to a distinguished collection of ancient and Islamic art as well as an exceptional collection of paintings, sculptures, and decorative arts from Europe.

3. The Berardo Collection Museum in Lisbon (Museu Coleço Berardo): This museum, which is housed in the Belém Cultural Center, has a sizable collection of modern artwork, including pieces by well-known creators including Picasso, Warhol, and Dal.

4. Ajuda National Palace in Lisbon (Palácio Nacional da Ajuda): In the nineteenth century, the royal home was this neoclassical building. It presently serves as a museum, displaying an extensive collection of fine arts, royal treasures, and historical art.

5. National Coach Museum (Museu Nacional dos Coches), Lisbon: This extraordinary museum has a remarkable collection of old royal carriages, including magnificent coaches used by Portuguese kings.

6. Lisbon's National Tile Museum (Museu Nacional do Azulejo) is home to Portugal's famous azulejos, or delicate ceramic tiles. This museum investigates the evolution of tile-making in Portugal across time.

7. museums are the Serralves Museum of Contemporary Art in Porto (Museu de Arte

Contemporânea de Serralves): This museum, housed at the Serralves Foundation, is surrounded by lovely gardens and parks and features contemporary art in a remarkable modernist structure.

8. National Machado de Castro Museum in Coimbra (Museu Nacional Machado de Castro): This museum, which is housed in a former bishop's palace, has an amazing collection of artwork and antiquities, including sculptures from the Roman, medieval, and Baroque periods.

9. National Museum Soares dos Reis, Porto: This museum in Porto has a varied collection of fine arts, decorative arts, and sculptures, with a focus on Portuguese art and artists.

10. Naval Museum in Lisbon, Museu de Marinha: This museum, which is situated in the Belém neighborhood, provides a fascinating look into Portugal's maritime history via the display of ship models, nautical equipment, and relics from the Age of Exploration.

11. Coimbra's National Machado de Castro Museum: The well-known Portuguese artist Joaquim Machado de Castro is honored with the name of this museum. It has a substantial collection of pottery, sculpture, and decorative arts.

12. The Museum of Contemporary Art Nadir Afonso in Chaves is a noteworthy example of contemporary art. The Portuguese painter Nadir Afonso is honored at this museum, which also features current works by other artists.

Travelers interested in learning more about Portugal's rich cultural past should not miss these museums and galleries, which provide a comprehensive picture of the country's artistic, cultural, and historical heritage. There are interesting museums and galleries to explore whether you're in Lisbon, Porto, Coimbra, or any other Portuguese city.

Parks And Gardens In Portugal

There are many beautiful parks and gardens in Portugal that highlight the nation's horticultural creativity, historical landscapes, and natural splendor. A sample of how stunning some of Portugal's parks and gardens are is given below:

Lisbon's Monsanto Forest Park (Parque Florestal de Monsanto): With hiking paths, picnic spots, and sweeping views of the city, Lisbon's Monsanto Forest Park is a sizable green space. The ideal getaway from the craziness of the city.

2. Pena Park in Sintra, often known as Parque da Pena: A verdant forest with meandering walkways, exotic plants, and secret grottoes surrounds Sinatra's famous Pena Palace in Pena Park. The park is a must-see because of its beautiful ambiance and vibrant vegetation.

3. Terra Nostra Park, Azores: Terra Nostra Park, a botanical park with an extensive variety of international species, is located on So Miguel Island in the Azores. The focal point is a sizable thermal pool where guests may unwind by swimming.

4. Crystal Palace Gardens in Porto (Jardins do Palácio de Cristal): These groomed gardens in Porto provide colorful flower beds, meandering walks, and a view of the Douro River. It's amazing to see the city and the river together.

5. In Madeira, the Monte Palace Tropical Garden (Jardim Tropical do Monte Palace) offers the following: There are tranquil lakes, unique flora from other continents, and sculptures with Asian influences in this verdant park on Madeira Island. It's breathtakingly lovely where you are, gazing over Funchal.

6. Braga's Bom Jesus do Monte: Famous for its enormous Baroque stairway and breathtaking grounds, the Bom Jesus do Monte sanctuary. Fountains, sculptures, and elaborate chapels embellish the tiered gardens.

7. Luso's Bussaco Forest (Mata Nacional do Buçaco): A protected area called Bussaco Forest is well-known for its gigantic sequoias and cedars as well as other old trees. Walking pathways, churches, and the magnificent Bussaco Palace Hotel may all be found in the forest.

8. Serralves Park (Parque de Serralves), Porto: Serralves Park (Parque de Serralves), Porto: The park surrounding the Serralves Foundation in Porto provides a combination of contemporary art installations, a lovely modernist home, and painstakingly planted gardens with a variety of plant species.

9. Jardim Botânico, Coimbra: This tranquil oasis is home to a vast range of flora, including rare and endangered species. Wander around its ponds, terraces, and shady paths.

10. Aveiro Salt Pans, also known as the Salinas de Aveiro: Instead of being conventional gardens, these salt pans are distinctive landscapes. A gorgeous image that is ideal for photography is created by the colorful salt flats and windmills.

A beautiful fusion of horticultural know-how, historical culture, and natural beauty may be found in Portugal's parks and gardens. You'll find a variety of lovely outdoor settings to discover and enjoy, whether you're exploring the well-kept gardens in Sintra, the verdant woods of the

Azores, or the urban parks in Lisbon and Porto.

Shopping in Portugal

Here are a few of Portugal's best locations for luxury shopping:

1. Lisbon's Avenida da Liberdade: Avenida da Liberdade is Lisbon's equivalent of Paris' Champs-Élysées. This tree-lined street is dotted with high-end shops from well-known labels like Louis Vuitton, Prada, and Gucci. It is the go-to place for designer clothing and accessories.

2. Porto Downtown: Elegant stores selling designer apparel, jewelry, and other upscale items may be found in Porto's historic center, particularly in the area surrounding Rua de Santa Catarina. El Corte Inglés, the most prominent department store in Portugal, is also nearby.

3. The Style Outlets in Lisbon: The Style Outlets, a

premium shopping experience featuring discounts on designer brands like Burberry, Michael Kors, and Boss, is situated just outside of Lisbon. It's the ideal location for clever consumers looking for expensive offers.

4. Designer Outlets: Designer outlet shops with huge savings on premium products can be found all around Portugal. Examples include the Freeport Fashion Outlet close to Lisbon and Vila do Conde The Style Outlets in Porto.

5. Principe Real, Lisbon: This fashionable area of Lisbon is well-known for its concept shops and upscale boutiques that carry local and foreign designers. It's a great location to get distinctive clothing and upscale household goods.

6. Chiado, Lisbon: Chiado is a posh shopping area in Lisbon that is home to multinational chains and upmarket businesses. It's a chic location for eating and shopping.

7. Joalharia do Carmo in Porto: is a renowned retailer that features magnificent items made by talented Portuguese jewelers. Joalharia do Carmo is a great place to shop for luxury jewelry in Porto.

Shopping on a Budget in Portugal:

While having access to upscale shopping is enticing, Portugal also offers fantastic options for those on a budget. There are a variety of places to buy that are reasonably priced and distinctive, from little markets to quaint boutiques:

1. Local Markets: Portugal is well-known for its vivacious and eye-catching local markets. If you're in Lisbon, Porto, or a smaller town, don't forget to browse the local markets for seasonal vegetables, unique handcrafted items, and vintage mementos.

2. Feira da Ladra, Lisbon: The Feira da Ladra,

often known as the "Thieves' Market," is Lisbon's first flea market. This place is a veritable gold mine of vintage, antique, and used products. It's a fantastic location to look for deals and unusual treasures.

3. Traditional crafts include the following: Portuguese pottery, cork goods, embroidered linens, and ceramic tiles (azulejos) are among the country's well-known traditional handicrafts. These genuine goods are available for purchase in regional artisan stores and marketplaces.

4. Lisbon's Neighborhoods: Lisbon's several neighborhoods provide distinctive shopping opportunities. While Graça and Bairro Alto provide distinctive boutiques and thrift stores, Alfama and Mouraria are home to inexpensive and lovely antique shops.

5. Porto's Markets: The Boho Market in Porto is a

crowded place to buy fresh fruit, spices, and Portuguese specialties. A fantastic location to get inexpensive seafood and regional cuisine is the Mercado do Porto.

Portugal boasts a booming fashion sector with alternatives that are within reach of most budgets. Look for Portuguese high-street retailers carrying fashionable apparel and accessories, such as ZARA, Mango, and Bershka.

6. Outdoor markets and events include: During your vacation, keep a look out for neighborhood festivals and outdoor markets. These gatherings often provide locally produced items, homemade crafts, and artisanal goods at affordable costs.

7. Souvenir stores: Souvenir stores in tourist locations provide a range of reasonably priced items, including Portuguese pottery and tiles as well as wine and cork goods. For the greatest bargains, don't forget to bargain a little.

8. Bookstores: Portugal has a vibrant literary legacy, and you can find several of them offering a variety of affordable works of classic and modern Portuguese literature.

9. Food markets include: Don't pass up the opportunity to peruse food stalls for inexpensive, delectable Portuguese delicacies. Try the local wines, cured meats, cheeses, and pastries.

8. Local Boutiques: Numerous little, independently owned boutiques and stores provide competitively priced apparel, accessories, and home furnishings. These shops often provide distinctive and adorable items.

Portugal offers both high-end shopping opportunities and reasonably priced retail therapy. Shopping in Portugal is an activity that suits all tastes, whether you're perusing upscale stores on Lisbon's Avenida da Liberdade or bargaining for a vintage discovery at Lisbon's Feira da Ladra.

Events and festivals in Portugal

Portugal is a dynamic nation that hosts a variety of events and festivals all year long to honor its rich cultural history. Visitors may get a taste of the nation's customs, music, dancing, and delectable cuisine during these events. Here is a sample of some of Portugal's most notable occasions and festivals, along with a list of related cultural events:

Fado music festivals include: Fado, the national music of Portugal, is an essential component of its culture. Fado events honor this depressing genre, such as the Amália Rodrigues Festival in Fundo and the Fado Museum Festival in Lisbon. Live Fado performances by well-known performers and up-and-coming talent will be provided for attendees.

Carnival (Carnaval): In Portugal, Carnival is celebrated with vibrant parades, loud street celebrations, and ornate costumes. The grandiose Carnival festivities in Lisbon and Loulé, which include samba dances, music, and processions, are well-known.

The So Joo Festival in Porto: One of the most eagerly awaited events in the nation is the So Joo Festival, which takes place in Porto on June 23. Bonfires, fireworks, and the custom of bashing one other over the head with toy hammers are all used to celebrate. The event features dancing, music, and street food.

Festival of Saint Joao in Braga: Another noteworthy festival of the Feast of St. John is the Festa de So Joo in Braga. The city is decked up in vibrant balloons and paper decorations, and there are concerts, street performances, and fireworks at midnight as part of the celebrations.

Festival of the Trays, Tomar (Festa dos Tabuleiros): In Tomar, there is a special festival known as the Festival of the Trays when young ladies carry enormous trays of bread and flowers on their heads. This occasion, which includes processions, singing, and dancing, blends religious and cultural components every four years.

Romaria (Religious Pilgrimages): The Romaria of Senhor da Pedra in Vila Nova de Gaia and the Pilgrimage of Our Lady of Fátima in Fátima are only a few of the religious pilgrimages that take place in Portugal every year. These occasions, which include processions, religious rites, and cultural performances, bring thousands of devoted pilgrims and visitors.

Fish and Flavors Festival in Lisbon (Peixe em

Lisboa): This culinary event in Lisbon honors the nation's seafood tradition. Visitors may participate in culinary demos, try a broad variety of seafood meals cooked by master chefs, and take in live entertainment.

Portugal Fashion: Portugal Fashion is a biennial exhibition of local fashion designers and up-and-coming designers held in Porto. Runway displays, exhibits, and cultural activities are all included, showcasing Portuguese fashion and design.

Sintra Music Festival: During the summer, the ancient town of Sintra hosts the Sintra Music Festival. It includes performances of classical music in renowned locations including the Monserrate Palace and the National Palace of Sintra.

Rock in Rio de Janeiro: Rock in Rio Lisboa, one of Portugal's biggest music events, brings together musicians from all over the world and the country. It lasts for many days and is jam-packed with entertainment, live music, and cultural events.

The Algarve International Fair (FIA) was held in 2011. The Algarve International Fair is a multicultural celebration of the area's variety that takes place every year in Faro. It offers a rich cultural experience by showcasing traditional music, dance, foods, and crafts from several countries.

Wine festivals include: Numerous wine festivals honor Portugal's vineyards and wine culture since the nation is well known for its wine. Events including wine tastings, parades, and cultural acts include the Douro Valley Wine Festival and the Madeira Wine Festival.

These celebrations and events in Portugal provide a fascinating fusion of musical styles, dancing movements, and gastronomic delights.

Portugal's festivals provide a superb chance to fully experience the rich culture of the nation, whether you're interested in traditional Fado music, exuberant street festivities, or delectable cuisine.

Portugal's nightlife

There is something for everyone in Portugal's nightlife, from club hoppers looking for busy clubs to those who prefer a more laid-back evening. Here is a sample of Portugal's vibrant nightlife scene and all it has to offer:

1. Nightlife in Lisbon:

Lisbon's ancient district of Bairro Alto comes to life at night. You may listen to a range of music, from electronic rhythms to Fado, on its winding streets, which are crowded with pubs and little clubs. Bar-hop and socialize with both locals and visitors.

Pink Street, also known as Rua Nova do Carvalho, is a popular destination for nightlife in Cais do Sodré.

It's a terrific spot to party all night long and sample some interesting drinks.

Fado Houses: Go to a Fado house for a more authentic taste of Portuguese nightlife. Enjoy supper and wine while listening to wonderful Fado music.

2. Nightlife in Porto:

Ribeira: This attractive nightlife destination is located along the Douro River. Take a stroll along the riverside and stop by bars for a drink or a glass of Porto wine.

Galerias de Paris: This Porto, Portugal, street is well-known for its vibrant nightlife. It's the perfect area to spend the evening with friends since there are several pubs and clubs there that play different kinds of music.

3. Nightlife in Algarve:

Albufeira: The Algarve region's seaside town is well-known for its thriving nightlife. The Strip, which has a variety of pubs and clubs, is the major core. Live music and DJs playing the newest hits are also available.

Beach Parties: Beach clubs and bars in the Algarve hold exciting events throughout the summer that have beachfront views and music that keeps you dancing till morning.

4. Dance and music:

Portugal is renowned for its love of dancing and music. In taverns and clubs all around the nation, live music performances range from classical Fado to contemporary pop and rock.

For fans of electronic music, Lisbon and Porto feature famous DJs and electronic music festivals that attract audiences from across the world.

5. Nighttime Eating:

After a night out, you may have a filling supper in one of the many Portuguese cities that provide late-night eating alternatives. Visit a nearby restaurant to sample some regional cuisine or indulge in a late-night snack.

Celebrations & Events:
Portugal has several festivals and events all year long, ranging from street celebrations to music festivals. Don't miss festivals like Santos Populares in June in Lisbon, when the streets come alive.

Views of the sunset:

The coastline of Portugal provides some stunning sunset vistas. At seaside bars, unwind with a glass of wine as you see the sun go below the horizon.

The nightlife in Portugal is not only about having fun; it's also about getting a taste of the rich social scene, music, and culture of the nation. Travelers looking for excitement and adventure after dark will never forget Portugal's nightlife, whether they're partying on the beach in the Algarve, dancing the night away in Porto, or exploring the ancient alleys of Lisbon.

CHAPTER 13

Top 15 hotels in Portugal

Of course, the following provides more thorough details on each of the hotels in Portugal:

1. The Yeatman in Porto, Portugal: Located in Vila Nova de Gaia, right over the river from Porto, The Yeatman is a high-end wine hotel. It provides breathtaking views of the Douro River and Porto's ancient city center. This five-star hotel is well-known for its wine-themed furnishings, vast wine cellars, and superb wine-tasting opportunities. It has a spa, a restaurant with a Michelin star, and exquisitely decorated rooms and suites. The Yeatman offers a unique chance to experience world-class luxury while being fully immersed in Portugal's wine culture.

2. The Six Senses Douro Valley: A tranquil hideaway surrounded by vineyards and the picturesque Douro River, Six Senses Douro Valley is located in the center of the Douro Valley. Beautifully built accommodations, a holistic spa, and farm-to-table cuisine are all included at this opulent eco-resort. Visitors may take part in numerous health and outdoor activities as well as tours of the wine area and wine tastings.

3. Hotel Memmo Baleeira in Sagres: A modern boutique hotel with a minimalist style, Memmo Baleeira Hotel is situated in Sagres on the southwest coast of Portugal. For people looking for peace and beauty in the natural world, it is the best option. The hotel provides wonderful ocean views, cozy lodgings, an outdoor pool, and quick access to the region's top beaches, including the well-known Praia do Beliche.

4. Penha Longa Resort near Sintra, Portugal: The luxurious Penha Longa Resort is located in the verdant Sintra Mountains. It has a spa, a championship golf course, and exquisitely designed gardens. The resort is renowned for its exquisite suites and accommodations as well as its top-notch cuisine. Visitors may visit the adjacent UNESCO World Heritage Sites in the medieval town of Sintra.

5. Lisbon's Santa Justa Hotel: In the center of Lisbon, next to the well-known Santa Justa Elevator, sits the boutique hotel Santa Justa. The hotel incorporates both contemporary and traditional Portuguese characteristics. It has cozy accommodations, a rooftop patio with expansive city views, and a chic restaurant. Many of Lisbon's attractions are easily accessible due to its central position.

6. The Lumiares in Lisbon, Portugal: A boutique hotel called The Lumiares is located in Lisbon's famed Bairro Alto district. It combines conventional Portuguese architecture with cutting-edge style. The hotel has trendy and comfortable lodgings, a rooftop bar with breathtaking city views, and a focus on regional and sustainable goods.

7. Hotel Torel Palace Porto: A lovely boutique hotel called the Torel Palace Porto Hotel is situated in Porto. It is renowned for its tranquil garden and distinctive, exquisitely furnished apartments. Travelers looking for a peaceful refuge in the city will love the hotel's quaint and pleasant ambiance.

8. The Four Seasons Hotel Ritz Lisbon: In the center of Lisbon, there is a renowned luxury hotel called the Four Seasons Hotel Ritz. Elegant guest rooms and suites, a rooftop fitness facility, and a collection of Portuguese artists' paintings are among its highlights. The Veranda restaurant of the hotel is renowned for its fine dining experiences.

9. Conrad Algarve: The Algarve area is home to the five-star luxury resort Conrad Algarve. It provides exquisite service, lovely suites and rooms, a lavish spa, and upscale dining selections. The resort is perfect for anyone looking for a mix of outdoor recreation and leisure along the Algarve coast.

10. The Vila Vita Parc Resort & Spa: A well-known luxury resort in the Algarve is Vila Vita Parc Resort & Spa. It has opulent guestrooms and suites, a variety of eating establishments, a private beach, and a wealth of spa amenities. The hotel is renowned for its superb customer service and breathtaking seaside setting.

11. The Cliff Bay is a 5-star hotel: in Funchal, Madeira, and is renowned for its stunning ocean views. It provides cozy accommodations, a restaurant with a Michelin star, and lovely grounds. Visitors may unwind by the infinity pool and take pleasure in the sea air.

12. Hotel Palácio da Bolsa in Porto: The old Palácio da Bolsa building in Porto houses this boutique hotel. With tastefully furnished rooms and convenient access to Porto's attractions, it provides a distinctive and stylish stay in the center of the city.

13. Tivoli Carvoeiro Algarve Resort:
located on the cliffs of the Algarve coast and giving breathtaking ocean views, is number thirteen. It offers cozy lodging, a variety of food choices, and access to lovely beaches.

14. The Pine Cliffs Hotel: a Luxury Collection Resort, is a well-known luxury resort in the Algarve recognized for its gorgeous golf courses, beachfront setting, and first-rate amenities.

15. Anantara Vilamoura Algarve Resort: This elegant Vilamoura resort provides an opulent hideaway with an emphasis on wellness, golf, and fine cuisine.

These hotels in Portugal provide a variety of luxurious experiences, from seaside getaways to city stays, each with its special charm and facilities. These hotels provide the ideal setting for your Portuguese vacation, whether you're looking for leisure, cultural discovery, or outdoor sports.

Low budget hotels in Portugal

Hostels, guesthouses, and low-cost hotels are just a few of the economical lodging choices Portugal has, making it affordable for visitors of all means. Here are a few inexpensive accommodations and choices in Portugal:

1. Portugal has a thriving hostel sector, notably in well-known tourist destinations like Lisbon, Porto, and Faro. Hostels provide inexpensive dormitory-style lodging and often feature community areas for meeting other visitors. Lisbon's Yes! Hostel, Porto's The Passenger Hostel, and Faro Boutique Hostel are three examples.

2. Guesthouses and Residences: Guesthouses and residencies are often family-run businesses that provide straightforward and inexpensive lodgings. They might range in terms of facilities and quality, but they are often an affordable choice for tourists. They may be found all across Portugal in various towns and cities.

3. Low-cost hotel brands: Portugal is home to several low-cost hotel businesses that provide luxurious lodging at fair rates. Ibis Budget, Travelodge, and easyHotel are a few well-liked choices with locations in several cities.

4. Vacation rentals and Airbnb: Private rooms, complete flats, and entire houses are just a few of the affordable alternatives available on Airbnb and other vacation rental websites. Families or groups who are traveling together may find this to be a cost-effective option.

5. Pousadas da Juventude (Youth Hostels): Pousadas da Juventude is a network of youth hostels in Portugal that offers inexpensive lodging for tourists of all ages. At reasonable prices, they provide both individual rooms and dormitory-style accommodations.

6. Albergues along the Camino of Santiago include: Along the Camino de Santiago, you may find inexpensive albergues (pilgrim hostels) if you're traveling through Portugal. These modest lodgings are ideal for individuals on a low budget and cater to pilgrims.

7. Small hotels and other accommodations in rural areas: Small inns and guesthouses with reasonable prices may be found in rural locations and small towns. These may provide a genuine and affordable experience.

8. Camping & Campsites: Portugal boasts a large number of campgrounds that welcome tent and RV campers. Camping is an affordable way to see the nation's natural splendor, particularly in regions like the Algarve and the Azores.

9. Off-Peak Travel: Consider going during the shoulder seasons or off-peak months since many lodgings have cheaper prices then. Cost reductions may also be attained by making reservations well in advance or by taking advantage of last-minute offers.

10. **Hostel organizations:** Hostel organizations exist in several Portuguese areas and provide details on inexpensive lodging options nearby. These organizations could provide members with discounts.

Read reviews and check booking sites for the most recent pricing and availability while searching for cheap hotels in Portugal. The greatest rates may be found by planning and being flexible with your vacation dates since costs might fluctuate based on the area and time of year.

Camping In Portugal

Portugal is a sanctuary for campers because of its varied landscapes and moderate temperature. Portugal has a plethora of chances to immerse yourself in the beauty of nature when camping, whether you're an expert camper or a beginner looking for outdoor adventure.

1. Numerous Camping Experiments:

Portugal accommodates a variety of camping tastes. Traditional campsites with well-kept amenities are an option, as are wild camping alternatives for a more primitive experience or glamping options for those looking for more comfort and luxury.

2. Magnificent Natural Environments:

The nation is blessed with a variety of natural beauty, from the clean beaches of the Algarve in the south to the verdant woods of Peneda-Gerês National Park in the north. Awakening to stunning views of mountains, rivers, lakes, and coastal cliffs is common for campers.

3. Camping by the sea:

There are several chances for beach camping throughout Portugal's wide coastline. Imagine waking up to the sight of the sun rising over the Atlantic Ocean after drifting off to sleep to the sound of waves. Camping sites may be found in areas with easy access to gorgeous beaches, such as Costa Vicentina and Cascais.

4. Retreats inland:

Consider setting up camp close to the magnificent Douro Valley wineries or in the Alentejo cork oak woods for a peaceful camping experience away from the ocean. These areas provide a tranquil setting for camping excursions.

5. Outdoor Recreation:

Camping in Portugal isn't only for relaxing; it's also for exploring. For campers who want to experience nature, hiking, mountain biking, bird viewing, and water sports like kayaking and surfing are popular pastimes.

6. Mild Weather

The majority of the year is suitable for camping in Portugal because of its Mediterranean climate. It's perfect to go camping in the spring and fall because of the pleasant weather and lack of summer visitors.

7. Security and laws:

Portugal has created strict camping laws to save its environment. Due to the danger of wildfires, wild camping is controlled, and campfires are often not allowed. Make careful you research local laws and get any required licenses.

8. Amenities at the campground:

Portugal's campgrounds normally include necessities like hygienic bathrooms, showers, power connections, and sometimes even on-site eating options. Many campsites welcome families and provide recreational opportunities.

9. Delights in Culture and Cuisine:

You may enjoy Portugal's delectable cuisine and rich culture by camping there. Discover regional markets, try regional cuisine, and interact with hospitable people to experience real Portuguese life.

10. Safety Advice

Although it is typically safe to camp in Portugal, it is still important to be mindful of your surroundings and use appropriate camping techniques. Respect nature, keep your campsite tidy, and adhere to any safety instructions issued by the campground management.

Camping in Portugal provides a unique outdoor experience, whether you like the rustic allure of wild camping or the conveniences of a well-equipped campsite. Portugal invites travelers to experience its natural treasures, moderate weather, and varied landscapes as they explore its campground by campsite. So gather your supplies, enjoy the serenity of nature, and make lifelong memories in this captivating European location.

CHAPTER 14

Top 15 Restaurants In Portugal

Portugal is known for its extensive culinary heritage, and a wide variety of restaurants provide delectable cuisine that highlights the national tastes. Here are 15 of Portugal's best restaurants, each famous for its own cuisine:

1. Belcanto, Lisbon: Chef José Avillez préparés avant-garde Portuguese cuisine at Belcanto, a two-star Michelin restaurant in Lisbon. Try the famous "Cantinho do Avillez," which combines codfish with coriander and chickpea purée.

2. Alma, Lisbon: Alma is a second Michelin-starred establishment in Lisbon that serves modern Portuguese cuisine. For a delicious fusion of tastes, try the "Bairrada suckling pig with cockles and seafood rice".

3. Eleven, Lisbon: Eleven is a Michelin-starred restaurant that specializes in contemporary Portuguese cuisine and offers breathtaking city views. Avoid skipping the "Lobster from the Berlenga Islands" or the "Alentejo Black Pork."

4. Feitoria, Lisbon: Feitoria is a Michelin-starred seafood restaurant that is housed in the Altis Belém Hotel. A good choice would be the "Algarve Lobster" or "Wild Sea Bass with Razor Clam."

5. Bon Bon, Carvoeiro: Bon Bon is a Michelin-starred restaurant serving modern Portuguese cuisine in Carvoeiro, Algarve. Take pleasure in meals like "Algarve fish and shellfish stew" or "Chocolate volcano."

6. Vila Joya: a two-star Michelin restaurant in Albufeira, offers a fusion of Portuguese and foreign cuisines. Pick up some "Black Pork Cheeks" or "Atlantic Sea Bass with Artichoke."

7. The Yeatman: a Michelin-starred restaurant in Porto, is well-known for its vast wine collection. Satisfy your appetite with delicacies like "Rice with Pig's Trotters and Cockles" or "Roasted Veal."

8. Antiqvvm, Porto: Antiqvvm is a restaurant with a Michelin star and a garden setting that looks out over Porto. Take pleasure in the "Octopus Carpaccio" or the "Iberian Pork with Mushrooms."

9. Fortaleza do Guincho, Cascais: Fortaleza do Guincho is a Michelin-starred restaurant that serves Portuguese food with a French influence and a seafood emphasis. Take a look at the "Grilled Turbot" or the "Suckling Pig."

10. The Ocean Restaurant, Alporchinhos: The Ocean Restaurant, which is part of Vila Vita Parc Resort & Spa, has two Michelin stars. Try the "Algarve Lobster" or the "Iberian Pork Pluma."

11. Lisbon's Tasca da Esquina: Portuguese tapas and small dishes are available at Tasca da Esquina in Lisbon for a more relaxed dining experience. Try the "Grilled Octopus" or the "Bacalhau à Brás."

12. Adega Vila Lisa, Sintra: Adega Vila Lisa is a popular spot for authentic Portuguese cuisine in Sintra. Try the duck rice or the clams in white wine and garlic known as "Amêijoas à Bulho Pato."

15. Cervejaria Ramiro in Lisbon, Portugal: is well known for its seafood, particularly its "Grilled Tiger Prawns" and "Bulhao Pato Clams."

14. O Gaveto, Matosinhos: O Gaveto, a restaurant in Matosinhos, is well known for its delicious fresh seafood, especially the "Seafood Rice" and the "Grilled Sea Bass."

15. A Cozinha do Manel, Porto: This little restaurant in Porto serves up traditional Portuguese cuisine. A substantial sandwich called the "Francesinha" or a stew called "Tripas à Moda do Porto" are also recommended.

Portugal's restaurants highlight the rich culinary legacy of the nation, showcasing everything from fine dining to regional specialties. These restaurants provide a broad selection of delicious treats to please your palette, whether you're a fan of seafood, Portuguese classics, or modern cuisine.

Coffee And Cafes Shops

For coffee lovers, Portugal provides a great experience with its rich coffee culture and lovely café settings. Portugal has plenty to offer any coffee enthusiast, whether they want a fast espresso shot or a leisurely sip while taking in the local atmosphere.

1.   Lisbon: The nation's capital is a great spot to begin your coffee exploration. Visit old areas like Alfama or Bairro Alto to uncover charming cafés hidden away in winding lanes. On a patio bathed in sunlight, sip a "Bica" (a Portuguese espresso) or a "café com leite" (coffee with milk) while taking in the sights of the city.

2. Porto: In the northern city of Porto, coffee connoisseurs may have a "cimbalino," which is comparable to an espresso but often served with some chocolate. For a morning pick-me-up, the Ribeira neighborhood along the Douro River offers delightful eateries with riverbank views.

3. Sintra: While visiting the charming town of Sintra, don't pass up the opportunity to have a cup of coffee at a typical Portuguese bakery. A delicious taste combination is a coffee and a "travesseiro," a local pastry filled with creamy almond cream.

4. Pastelarias: You can find pastelarias, or pastry stores, almost everywhere in Portugal. These are great locations to sip coffee and nibble something delicious. Try a "galo" (coffee with a lot of milk) and a "pastel de nata," a well-known custard pastry from Portugal.

5. Café A Brasileira (Lisbon): For more than a century, intellectuals, creative types, and coffee enthusiasts have congregated at this iconic café in the center of Lisbon. Enjoy your coffee while gazing at the statue of Fernando Pessoa, one of Portugal's best poets.

6. Café Majestic (Porto): This Belle Époque masterpiece is regarded as one of the world's most magnificent eateries. Enjoy a coffee in the sumptuous setting and experience a sense of time travel.

7. Algarve: Enjoy your coffee with a view of the

Atlantic Ocean as you unwind at seaside cafés along the breathtaking southern coastline. It is energizing to drink fragrant coffee when the sea air is blowing.

8.   specialty   Coffee Shops: Lisbon and Porto in particular are seeing a rise in the popularity of specialty coffee shops as the Portuguese coffee landscape changes. These locations offer to people looking for a distinctive coffee experience by focusing on premium beans and brewing techniques.

Portugal's coffee culture provides a lovely fusion of tastes and settings, whether you favor the historic allure of classic cafés or the contemporary flare of specialized coffee shops. So take your time, enjoy each cup, and become lost in this lovely country's enticing café culture.

CHAPTER 15

Top 15 local Cuisines to try in Portugal

Portugal has a wide variety of delectable regional cuisines that showcase the nation's extensive gastronomic history. Here are 15 must-try Portuguese foods along with instructions on how to make them:

1. Bacalhau à Brás : In Portuguese cooking, codfish that has been salted is known as bacalhau. Codfish is sliced into little pieces and cooked with straw fries and finely chopped onions to make bacalhau à brás. Black olives and fresh parsley are used as garnishes, while scrambled eggs are used as a binding agent.

2. Pastéis de Nata: Famous Portuguese custard pastries are called pastéis de Nata. A creamy custard consisting of

242

eggs, sugar, and milk is placed into the flaky pastry shell, which is then cooked until a caramelized top appears. They often have powdered sugar and cinnamon sprinkled on top.

3. Feijoada a la Transmontana:
The Trás-os-Montes area is home to the hearty bean stew known as feijoada à Transmontana. It includes a variety of pork slices cooked with white beans and flavorful spices, including sausages, ribs, and sometimes even pig's ears and trotters.

4. Cozido à Portuguesa: Cozido à Portuguesa is a typical stew from Portugal. It often consists of a variety of meats, such as pig, beef, and sausages, as well as vegetables including potatoes, cabbage, and carrots. Rich tastes are developed by prolonged cooking.

5. Arroz de Pato: Arroz de Pato is a rice dish made with duck in Portugal. After marinating, the duck is grilled till tender. Rich and savory rice is produced when the rice is cooked in the aromatic fat and stock of the duck.

6. Francesinha: This filling sandwich is a specialty of Porto. It is made up of layers of cheese, steak, and cured meats (such ham and linguiça) that are all topped in a hot tomato and beer sauce. Regularly, it comes with a side of French fries.

7. Açorda: Açorda is a typical bread stew from Portugal. It is prepared by soaking crusty bread in a delicious broth consisting of herbs, garlic, and olive oil. Poached eggs and fresh coriander may be added as garnishes.

8. Amêijoas à Bulhão Pato, number: Amêijoas à Bulhão Pato is a well-known clam dish from Portugal. The clams are prepared in a white wine and olive oil-based sauce that is garlicky and lemony. Fresh coriander provides a flavorful kick.

9. Arroz de Tamboril: This rice dish, which includes monkfish, is called arroz de Tamboril. To create a tasty and fragrant seafood meal, the fish is cooked with rice, tomatoes, onions, and aromatic spices.

10. Leitão à Bairrada: This regional specialty comes from the Bairrada area. It includes a flavorful roasted piglet that has been salted and garlic-seasoned. Even though the flesh is still soft and tasty, the skin becomes crunchy.

11. Caldo Verde: Caldo Verde is a typical green soup from Portugal. It is prepared with potatoes, pieces of Portuguese chouriço sausage, and thinly sliced collard greens in a broth seasoned with garlic and olive oil.

12. Carne de Porco à Alentejana: A meal from the Alentejo area é carne de porco à Alentejana. Clams and seasoned pork cubes are combined in a tasty white wine, paprika, and garlic sauce. Fried potatoes are often included with it.

13. Amêijoas à Algarvia, number: Clams are cooked with garlic, onions, white wine, and fresh herbs in a meal called amêijoas à Algarvia. It's a simple yet delicious seafood meal that highlights the regional tastes of the Algarve.

14. Polvo à Lagareiro: Roasted octopus is served with plenty of garlic, extra virgin olive oil, and crispy potatoes in Polvo à Lagareiro. Before roasting, the octopus is tenderized, making for a tasty and tender meal.

15. Sardinhas Assadas, or grilled sardine:, are often served with a drizzle of olive oil and a dusting of sea salt. They are particularly popular in the summers during Portuguese festivities and celebrations.

These are only a few of the many mouth watering delicacies you may eat in

Portugal. It is a pleasant gastronomic trip to explore the local food since each area of the nation has its unique peculiarities.

CHAPTER 16

10-days Itinerary

Portugal's varied landscapes, rich history, energetic towns, and delectable food may all be explored within a 10-day tour. A thorough itinerary covering some of Portugal's most famous locations is provided below:

Arrival in Lisbon on the first day

- Touch down in Lisbon, the nation of Portugal. After your trip, check into your hotel and unwind.
- Take a walk around the old Alfama neighborhood in the evening and have supper at a typical Fado restaurant.

Day 2's Exploration of Lisbon

- Begin your day by traveling to Belém, where you may see the Jerónimos Monastery and sample the renowned Pastéis de Nata at Pastéis de Belém.
- Take time to explore the Monument to the Discoveries and the Belém Tower.
- Visit stores, cafés, and attractions like the So Jorge Castle in the Baixa and Chiado neighborhoods throughout your afternoon. Dine out at the renowned Bairro Alto neighborhood.

Day 3: a day trip to Sintra

- Visit the UNESCO World Heritage site of Sintra on a day excursion.
- View the magnificent Pena Palace and stroll through Sinatra's old town.

- The Quinta da Regaleira and the Moorish Castle should not be missed.
- For supper, go back to Lisbon in the evening.

Day 4: Lisbon to Porto

- Take a train or a flight to Porto, the second-largest city in Portugal.
- In the afternoon, spend some time visiting the famed Ribeira neighborhood along the Douro River after checking into your accommodation. Taste some of Porto's world-famous wine while you have supper at a riverbank restaurant.

Day 5: Exploration of Porto

- Explore the historic center, taking in the Clerigos Tower and So Bento Railway Station, as well as Livraria Lello, one of the most stunning bookshops in the world. Enjoy a meal of classic Portuguese fare like Francesinha while taking a river boat down the Douro to see the city's bridges and cellars.

Day 6: Douro Valley

- Spend a day excursion seeing the Douro Valley, which is renowned for its terraced vineyards and winemaking.
- Take a tour and wine tasting at a nearby vineyard.
- Take in the beautiful surroundings along the Douro River.
- In the evening, return to Porto.

Day 7: Porto to Coimbra

- Visit Coimbra, which is the location of one of Europe's oldest universities.
- Visit the Joanina Library and see the university's historic campus.
- Dine in a classic Portuguese restaurant

while strolling around the quaint Old Town.

Day 8: Travel from Coimbra to Évora.

- Leave for Évora, an exquisitely preserved medieval town in the Alentejo area.
- Inquire about visiting the Chapel of Bones and the Roman Temple of Évora.
- Take in a local Alentejo meal while exploring the old city center.

Day 9:

- On the way back from Évora to Lisbon make a stop at the village of Setbal.
- Lunch may be had at a neighborhood restaurant in Setbal with fresh fish.
- Spend your day touring Vasco da Gama Shopping Center and Lisbon's contemporary Parque das Nações. In Lisbon, have a goodbye meal.

Day 10 is the departure day.

- Depending on the time of your flight, you could have some extra time for last-minute shopping or sightseeing.
- Bring back great memories of your 10-day journey to Portugal as you depart from Lisbon.

This schedule provides a thoughtful combination of opportunities for historical research, scenic beauty, and gastronomic pleasures. Of course, Portugal has more to offer, so feel free to alter your plans based on your tastes and areas of interest. Have fun traveling around this fascinating nation!

<u>CONCLUSION</u>

Traveling through the alluring countries of Spain and Portugal is like entering a novel where history, culture, and the natural world come together in a perfect dance. The echoes of flamenco rhythms, the fragrance of freshly brewed coffee in charming Lisbon cafés, and the breath-taking vistas of old Alhambra castles stay in your mind as your journey through these magical nations comes to an end, weaving an unforgettable tapestry of memories.

With its many areas, each of which offers a distinct taste of Spanish history, Spain has become a treasure trove for tourists. Spain astonishes at every turn, from the architectural marvels of Gaudi in Barcelona to the impassioned energy of Andalusia's flamenco. In museums like the Prado and the Reina Sofia, the thriving city of Madrid displays its cultural treasures, while Seville charms visitors with its majestic Alcazar and the aroma of orange blossoms in the air. Valencia's contemporary City of Arts and Sciences contrasts with the historic old town's timeless appeal, resulting in an enthralling fusion of the two eras.

Portugal provides a more tranquil but no less alluring experience with its soul-stirring fado music and gentle Atlantic breezes. Lisbon encourages you to get lost in its old-world beauty with its pastel-colored buildings and curvy streets. The Douro Valley's visual appeal, which is enhanced by terraced vineyards, provides a stunning representation of the nation's wine-making heritage. Porto, a city of wine cellars and ancient alleyways, perfectly encapsulates Portugal's maritime past.

Both countries have a love of delicious food that entices the palate. A gastronomic journey is created by Spain's tapas, paella, and superb wines from the Priorat and Rioja regions. In Portugal, enjoying seafood feasts, indulging in creamy pastéis de nata, and drinking world-famous port wine along the Douro River become treasured memories.

The warmth of the people, more than the culinary wonders and architectural wonders, is what makes a lasting impact. Every contact is a meaningful experience because of the villagers' genuine warmth and eagerness to introduce visitors to their culture.

As you say goodbye to these remarkable places, you take with you more than just photos and trinkets; you also have a strong feeling of connection to Spain's and Portugal's rich history and admiration for their dynamic presence. The Iberian Peninsula is charming not only because of its landmarks and scenery but also because of how it makes you feel, like a welcome visitor amid a rich tapestry of history and modernity. Therefore, when your tour comes to an end, think back on the Atlantic Ocean sunsets, the conversations had in tapas restaurants, and the enduring attraction of ancient alleyways. With their distinct histories, Spain and Portugal will stand as a monument to the wonder of travel and the skill of exploration in your heart .

Made in the USA
Coppell, TX
07 November 2023